W9-ADX-828

World Writers

PRIZE WINNERS
Ten Writers for Young Readers

Penelope Yunghans

MORGAN
REYNOLDS
Incorporated

Greensboro

PRIZE WINNERS *Ten Writers for Young Readers*

Copyright © 1995 by Penelope Yunghans

Library of Congress Cataloging-in-Publication Data
Yunghans, Penelope, 1946-
    Prize winners : ten writers for young readers / Penelope Yunghans.
        p.   cm. -- (World writers)
    Includes bibliographical references (p.   ) and index.
    Contents: Beverly Cleary -- Roald Dahl -- Madeleine L'Engle -- Betsy Byars --
Jean Little -- Katherine Paterson -- Richard Peck -- Virginia Hamilton --
Walter Dean Meyers -- Gary Paulsen.
    ISBN   1-883846-11-0
        1. Authors, American--20th century--Biography--Juvenile literature.   2. Children's
literature, American--Bio-bibliography--Juvenile literature.   I. Title II. Series
PS490. Y86   1995
810. 9 ' 9282—dc20
[B]

95-37990
CIP

Printed in the United States of America

First Edition

CONTENTS

BEVERLY CLEARY
An Ordinary Girl

Six-year-old Beverly Bunn stamped her feet, cried, and threw her book on the floor. Learning to read was so hard! And reading was boring!

"Why couldn't authors write about the sort of boys and girls who lived on my block? Why couldn't authors skip all that tiresome description and write books in which something happened on every page? Why couldn't they make the stories funny?"

By the time Beverly was eight years old she had discovered that books could be fun. And what's more, she wanted to be an author when she grew up. She knew exactly what kind of books she would write, too—funny books, in which lots of things happened to plain, ordinary boys and girls.

Beverly Bunn Cleary did just that. She wrote more than seventy books about children like the ones she grew up with in Portland, Oregon. She received over sixty awards for her writing, and her home town honored her by placing statues of some of her most popular characters in a park near Klickitat Street in Portland, where some of the scenes in her books take place.

Beverly was born on April 12, 1916. An only child, she spent her first six years on a farm in Yamhill, Oregon. It was not an easy life—the family had very little money and her parents worked hard. The farm was lonely, the house large and cold, and the work endless. She once heard her mother complain, "For me, those were years of slavery."

Beverly's mother was a former teacher. She taught Beverly to love literature, and was always quoting her favorite authors—Geoffrey Chaucer and Charles Dickens. Her mother enjoyed telling Beverly stories such as "Little Red Riding Hood," "The Three Little Pigs," "Chicken Little," and "The Little Red Hen."

Beverly owned only two books as a pre-schooler—*Mother Goose* and *The Story of the Three Bears.* She heard them so often she learned them by heart. She also had favorites from her mother's library: a collection of fairy tales and Beatrix Potter's *The Tailor of Gloucester.* Potter's book inspired her to learn embroidery. "My stitches never matched those of the mice in *The Tailor of Gloucester,* but I discovered how soothing handwork could be."

One of her first adventures with handwork involved an irresistibly appealing white damask tablecloth. Beverly poured ink onto one end of the cloth, dipped her hands into it and walked around the table, marking the cloth with small blue handprints. How satisfying it was to cover that white surface with imprints of her hands!

Another time Beverly's father was butchering a hog in the yard. Beverly had been told she could not go outside to watch. Like most farm children, Beverly understood the importance of obeying safety rules, but she really wanted to see the butchering. Her solution was to watch from an upstairs window.

As she leaned out, she spied a narrow ledge just below the window. The ledge went all the way around the house. It seemed to Beverly that it would be fun and quite easy to circle the house on this ledge. She climbed out the window to try it. Her parents spotted her from below and they ran to her rescue. Beverly didn't understand their panic. She was sure she wouldn't have fallen.

Beverly attributes her confidence to her mother, who often told her, "Never be afraid." Beverly was not only fearless, she was constantly active. "Grandpa sometimes paid me a nickel to sit still for five minutes," she bragged.

When Beverly was six years old, her father decided to give up farming. He grew good crops, but received little money for them. Although he loved the active outdoor life, the family would be better off if he found work in Portland.

Beverly was happy to move. She looked forward to living on a street with other children, going to school, and learning to read. She wanted to learn to read with the other children in school, and would not let her mother teach her.

The Bunns moved to a neighborhood full of children. Beverly loved rollerskating, making "stilts" of two-pound tin cans tied on with string, and playing "brick factory," a game in which kids pounded bricks into dust.

She and her mother made frequent trips to the library where they found *The Blue Bird*, by Maurice Maeterlinck. The story was about two children who looked for the bluebird of Happiness. After reading it, her mother said, "It's true...we find happiness in our own back-yard." Beverly agreed. She was happy in Portland, and was eager for school to begin.

Although she wanted to learn to read, Beverly was anxious. Would the teacher like her? As things turned out, Beverly didn't like the teacher. She thought she was too strict. Sometimes Beverly was punished when she was not even sure what she had done wrong. She became afraid to go to school.

When her mother visited to see why Beverly was so unhappy, the teacher acted very kind and gentle. Commenting on how nice the teacher was, Mrs. Bunn insisted that Beverly should remember her "pioneer ancestors" and be brave.

Beverly thinks that her early reading problems were caused by fear of this teacher. The next year, when she had a cheerful and affectionate teacher, she learned to read well. Still, she refused to read outside of school. For some reason, she felt that reading should be confined to the classroom. She enjoyed being read to, however. Her favorite books that year were George MacDonald's fantasies, *The Princess and the Goblin* and *The Princess and Curdie.*

Beverly was bored one day during the third grade. Leafing through a book her mother had brought home for her, her attention was caught by the adventures of *The Dutch Twins*, a book by Lucy Fitch Perkins. At the library she found other books in the "Twins" series, and was excited to discover she was able to read these interesting stories by herself. The boring readers used in school had misled her into thinking reading would never be fun. Beverly began reading almost instantly.

Mr. Bunn was unhappy as a bank guard. The job was dull and his feet hurt from standing on hard marble floors all day. It was a financial improvement over farming, but the family still struggled. They had little money for household expenses. The house was often chilly because they couldn't afford firewood. Beverly's friends didn't like to visit her in this cold, drab house, where her mother was always tired and nervous.

Of course, there was little money for extras. Beverly received an allowance of ten cents a week that she had to save until there was enough to buy what she wanted.When she saw the stage version of *Peter Pan*, she loved the pirates and wanted to buy the book. It took her weeks to save the money.

The library became Beverly's refuge from the dreariness of home. It was a warm, peaceful place with wicker furniture and beautiful paintings where she could read for hours. She enjoyed mysteries, humorous stories about real people, fairy tales with comfortable happy endings, and Greek myths. A favorite was the story of Persephone and her mother, Demeter. Beverly found comfort in this story about the absence of spring and a mother's search for her daughter. "I came to understand that we cannot expect flowers to bloom continuously in life."

Beverly's writing career began in third grade. A local newspaper offered a free book to any child who wrote a book review. Her mother took her to the newspaper office where she was given a copy of *The Story of Dr. Doolittle* by Hugh Lofting. She enjoyed the book. Her review, along with her picture, appeared in the *Oregon Journal*. Several of Beverly's schoolmates said they had seen her picture, but she was disappointed that no one mentioned having read her book review.

In fourth grade, Beverly won $2.00 for an essay on the beaver—Oregon's state animal. She later discovered that no one else had entered the contest. It was a valuable lesson—Beverly realized that successful people are the one's who are willing to try.

By this time Beverly knew she wanted to be a writer, and she was encouraged by her teachers. Sometimes the lessons she learned were not what the teachers intended. One school assignment was to write a descriptive paragraph. Beverly's paper was returned covered with the teacher's corrections. Beverly learned a lesson from this, too. When she writes her books, she puts in very little description. Some of her readers tell her that's one of the things they like most about her books.

Teachers in Beverly's day seldom praised their students for fear of spoiling them. However, they often returned Beverly's stories with compliments on her humor and talent. Beverly's class was once assigned an essay about a favorite book character. Beverly had so many favorites, she couldn't choose. Instead, she wrote "A Journey Through Bookland" about a girl who interviews all the characters she meets during an imagined trip through her favorite novels. The teacher later told the class, "When Beverly grows up, she should write children's books."

Such encouragement convinced Beverly that she would become an author. She even found the location on the school library shelves where her books would one day reside.

Beverly continued to receive praise for her writing. When she was a high school freshman, her first story was published in the school newspaper. Unfortunately, someone else was listed as the author. Although a correction was printed in the next issue, some of the excitement was taken away. That story, much revised, later appeared in Beverly's first book.

As a sophomore, Beverly received a grade of Fair—the lowest grade she had ever received—on a story outline. The completed story received a grade of Excellent. Here was another writing lesson. Beverly doesn't bother to outline her fiction. She starts writing, employing her imagination freely. Then she rewrites and revises until she has all the events of the story in the right order, and is satisfied with the result.

These were the years of the Great Depression. Many people lost their jobs. Businesses closed. Soup kitchens were opened to feed the unemployed. The homeless gathered together in makeshift camps named "Hoovervilles" after President Herbert Hoover, who was charged with a lack of sympathy for the poor.

Beverly's father lost his bank job in the summer of 1930. He had few qualifications for city work, and jobs were very scarce. Mrs. Bunn looked for work also, but was unable to find any.

The Bunns economized in every way possible. Mrs. Bunn used almond extract in almost everything she baked because it was cheaper than other flavorings. They cancelled the *Saturday Evening Post*, which had been a favorite magazine. Mr. Bunn gave up his pipe and sold his car. He was proud of making a razor blade last for a year by sharpening it on the inside of a straight-edged drinking glass. Beverly took sewing in high school so that she could make her own clothes.

But poverty created pressure, and tension mounted between Beverly's parents. She escaped the gloom of the house as often as she could to go window shopping or to the library.

Mr. Bunn finally found a job as manager of the safety-deposit vault in a bank. He made less money than before, and for a man who loved outdoor activities, it was hard to work all day in a windowless basement. Beverly said, "I felt as if he were serving a sentence, condemned to support Mother and me."

In spite of their financial problems, Beverly's parents were reluctant to have her look for work. Many of her friends found summer jobs picking fruit, but Beverly was not allowed to join them. Nor was she permitted to work as a cashier in one of the city's large department stores.

Beverly did accept a babysitting job the summer of her junior year. For fifty cents a day, she spent an afternoon washing dishes, shelling peas, vacuuming, and babysitting a two-year-old. The child's mother returned home before the vacuuming was done, but Beverly was not allowed to leave until she finished the job. "I was paid a pittance trying to do two jobs at once in someone's dirty kitchen....I wanted a real job or I wanted to be left alone to lie on my bed in my room and read Willa Cather."

After that terrible job, Beverly was delighted to be invited by her friend Claudine to spend part of the summer at a family camp in the country. There Beverly and Claudine hiked, swam, and read Sigrid Undset's *Kristin Lavransdatter* to each other.

At the end of that relaxing vacation, Beverly returned to the strict atmosphere of her home. Her mother had a long list of rules:

> Always sift cake flour before measuring.
> Windows washed when the sun is shining will streak.
> Reading is to the mind as exercise is to the body.
> Always try to make the world a better place.

It felt like constant criticism. She wondered if she would ever be able to do anything right in her mother's eyes.

Beverly often wished her mother were more affectionate. She remembers being kissed by her mother only once, after she came home from a friend's house and announced, "Some mothers kiss their little girls." She had a tonsillectomy at the age of eleven. When she woke up after the operation, she was surprised to hear her mother call her "sweetheart." It was the only time her mother ever called her by an endearing name.

Beverly was not allowed to make many decisions for herself, even when she was in high school. Her mother attempted to control Beverly's friendships, her style of clothes, and even her college plans. Beverly felt her mother wanted to live through her because she had no other interests.

Beverly's father finally stepped in to help his daughter achieve her independence. When a cousin in southern California invited Beverly to live with her for two years while attending tuition-free Chaffee Junior College, Mrs. Bunn objected. However, Mr. Bunn insisted that Beverly should accept. Beverly was eager. After worrying about college costs all through high school, here was the opportunity she had been hoping for—the chance to continue her education and realize her dream of becoming a writer.

After receiving her associate's degree from Chaffee, Beverly earned a bachelor's degree from the University of California at Berkeley. Then, not sure that she could support herself by writing, she decided that she needed a steady way of earning a living. She remembered the inviting, quiet library she had loved as a girl, and decided to be a librarian. She earned her degree in library science from the University of Washington. In 1939, Beverly became the children's librarian for the public library in Yakima, Washington.

In 1940, Beverly married Clarence Cleary. They moved to Oakland, California, where Beverly served as the post librarian at the U. S. Army Hospital from 1943 to 1945.

When World War II ended, the Clearys moved to a house in the hills around Berkeley, California. When they discovered several reams of typing paper left behind by the previous owners, Beverly announced that she would write a book if only she had a sharp pencil. The next day Clarence brought home a pencil sharpener, and Beverly set out to fulfill her dream of becoming an author. She wrote a funny book about the neighborhood she had grown up in. She named the main character Henry Huggins.

Beverly heard an editor from the William Morrow Publishing Company speak at a conference. The editor looked like someone she would like to read her manuscript, so she sent it to him. She soon received a letter from the editor saying they would like to publish her book, and asking her to make some minor changes in the last chapter. Beverly agreed, and *Henry Huggins* was published in 1950. It has been followed by book after book about "plain, ordinary boys and girls."

Beverly begins writing most of her books on the second of January, the date *Henry Huggins* was started. She still does not start with an outline. Instead, she just thinks of a character and several incidents. She has no clear idea of what the storyline will be until she begins to write. Discovering what is going to happen to her characters is part of the fun.

Many of Beverly's books draw upon incidents from her own childhood and from the experiences of her twin son and daughter,

Malcolm and Marianne. Henry Huggins and his friends Ellen Tebbits, Otis Spofford, Beezus and Ramona Quimby all live on Klickitat Street—the name of a real street in Beverly's Portland, Oregon neighborhood. Ellen Tebbits was forced to wear hated woolen underwear. Beverly was too. Ramona Quimby was referred to by a teacher as a nuisance. Beverly was too. Ellen Tebbits was cast as a substitute rat in a school play. Beverly was a substitute lilac blossom. In *Ramona and her Mother*, the phrase, "Oh, you silly little girls" echoes a favorite saying of Claudine's mother. Otis Spofford's garlic-eating, Henry Huggins' tin soldier, the trouble that twins Mitch and Amy have with the multiplication tables, all have their origins in Beverly's childhood experiences.

In 1984, Beverly's novel *Dear Mr. Henshaw* won the Newbery Award. This award is given annually by the American Library Association for "the most distinguished contribution to children's literature."

The idea for *Dear Mr. Henshaw* came from children's letters. Like Leigh Botts in the book, many children write to Beverly asking for answers to long lists of questions. Often they tell her they will get extra credit in school if she answers their letters. Beverly says she is sometimes tempted to respond with a list of questions for them.

Many of the letters she receives from her readers are funny, or sad, or make her think. Several boys had asked her to write a book about a boy whose parents were divorced. Beverly combined this idea with the comment she heard a woman make about an absent father who promised to call his son but didn't. She also used an incident a teacher described about a boy who rigged a loud burglar alarm in his lunchbox. All of these ideas found their way into *Dear Mr. Henshaw*.

When she contemplated a writing career during her high school years, Beverly wondered what she would write about. She was "ordinary"—could she depend on her pen and her imagination for a living? For almost fifty years Beverly Cleary has been proving that she most certainly can. She writes exactly the sort of books she always said she would—funny books, in which lots of things happen to plain, ordinary boys and girls.

Notes:

Page 11   "Why couldn't authors write..." Anne Commire, ed., *Something About the Author* (Gale Research Co., 1986), vol. 43, p. 54.

"For me, those were..." Beverly Cleary, *A Girl from Yamhill* (William Morrow and Company, Inc., 1988), p. 109.

Page 12   "My stitches never matched..." Cleary, *A Girl from Yamhill*, p.119.

Page 13   "Never be afraid." Cleary, *A Girl from Yamhill*, p. 39.

"Grandpa sometimes..." Cleary, *A Girl from Yamhill*, p. 53.

Page 14   "It's true..." Cleary, *A Girl from Yamhill*, p. 73.

"Pioneer ancestors" Cleary, *A Girl from Yamhill*, p. 83.

Page 15   "I came to understand..." Cleary, *A Girl from Yamhill*, p. 125.

Page 16   "When Beverly grows up..." Cleary, *A Girl from Yamhill*, p. 147.

Page 18   "I felt as if..." Cleary, *A Girl from Yamhill*, p. 253.

"I was paid..." Cleary, *A Girl from Yamhill*, p. 239.

Always sift... Cleary, *The Horn Book Magazine*, (August, 1984), p. 430.

Page 19   "Some mothers kiss..." Cleary, *A Girl from Yamhill*, p. 113.

For further reading
about Beverly Cleary:

Cleary, Beverly. *A Girl from Yamhill.* New York: William Morrow and Company, Inc., 1988

"Newbery Medal Acceptance Speech." *The Horn Book Magazine,* August 1984.

Commire, Anne, ed. *Something About the Author.* Detroit: Gale Research Company, 1986, Vol. 43.

Books for Young Readers by Beverly Cleary

1950	Henry Huggins
1951	Ellen Tebbits
1952	Henry and Beezus
1953	Otis Spofford
1954	Henry and Ribsy
1955	Beezus and Ramona
1956	Fifteen
1957	Henry and the Paper Route
1958	The Luckiest Girl
1959	Jean and Johnny
1961	Emily's Runaway Imagination
1961	Sister of the Bride
1962	Henry and the Clubhouse
1965	The Mouse and the Motorcycle
1967	Mitch and Amy
1973	Socks
1975	Ramona the Brave
1977	Ramona and Her Father
1979	Ramona and Her Mother
1981	Ramona Quimby, Age Eight
1981	Runaway Ralph
1982	Ralph S. Mouse
1982	Ramona the Pest
1982	Ribsy

1983   Dear Mr. Henshaw

1984   Lucky Chuck

1985   Ramona Forever

1986   The Real Hole

1986   Two Dog Biscuits

1987   The Growing-Up Feet

1988   Janet's Thingamajigs

1990   Muggie Maggie

1992   Strider

1993   Petey's Bedtime Story

ROALD DAHL
Accomplishing Important Things

Roald and his sister rode their tricycles at top speed down the middle of the street, taking the corner on two wheels. It was 1922, and cars were rare in the small village of Llandaff—the street belonged to the children racing each other to school. As an adult, Roald remembered nothing else of that year in kindergarten, but he remembered those races with Alfhild.

"Great excitement is probably the only thing that really interests a six-year-old boy—and it sticks in his mind."

Roald Dahl was born in Wales on September 13, 1916, the son of Norwegian immigrants. When Roald was three years old his seven-year-old sister Astrid died suddenly from appendicitis. Not long afterwards, his father, sick with grief for his beloved daughter, fell ill with pneumonia and died. Sofie Dahl, Roald's mother, was left with four children of her own and two stepchildren to raise. She was urged by her family to return to Norway where they could help her, but she remained in Great Britain, knowing the children's father had wanted them to have an English education.

At the age of five, Roald entered Elmtree House, the little village kindergarten. After one year there, he went to Llandaff Cathedral School where the headmaster seemed to him like a giant in a tweed suit and black gown. In well-to-do English families at that time it was customary to send boys away to boarding school, so when Roald was nine years old he entered St. Peter's school in Somerset, England.

It was hard for Roald to leave home, where he was known as "the Apple," because he was his mother's favorite child—the "apple of her eye." St. Peter's was strict; caning was the punishment for breaking any of the many rules. Roald was so homesick his first term he faked illness so that he would be sent home to recover.

But school and separation from home were unavoidable, and Roald learned to cope. He determined in which direction home lay, and found comfort by sleeping facing that direction. He also wrote to his mother every week. Letter-writing became a habit. He continued to write to his mother weekly—sometimes more often—unitl she died forty-two years later.

Roald got along fairly well with the other boys and was good at games, but his grades were weak. Probably because he spent most of his time reading adventure stories.

On Saturday mornings Roald and the other students gathered in the school assembly hall. There they listened to a lecture on England's vast literary heritage. The talks were given by a woman who turned these sessions into the most positive experience Roald had at this school. He learned to appreciate good writing as England's most important authors were discussed, and selections from their works read aloud.

During summer vacations the Dahl family traveled to Norway to visit relatives in Oslo. Here Roald was introduced to Norwegian tales of witches and trolls which captured his imagination and inspired much of his later writing. The family traveled by boat down the Oslo fjord to a small island, where they stayed at a hotel and spent their days boating, swimming, and fishing. The holidays were idyllic and Roald reveled in the family life which he missed so much during the school term.

When Roald was thirteen years old he entered Repton, another boarding school. Here he established himself as an athlete, becoming a valued team member in several sports. But Roald was not happy at Repton. He considered the uniform he had to wear ridiculous. The cutaway coat, striped trousers, and straw hat made him feel "like an undertaker's apprentice in a funeral parlor."

Repton's very strict rules were enforced by beatings, often administered by the older boys. Although Roald never wanted to be one of the school officers whose job it was to punish rule-breakers, he was sometimes a bully—teasing and making up cruel nicknames for fellow students. Roald had a strong rebellious streak. He chafed under the many strict rules. He missed his home. He disliked his classes. His verbal attacks on other boys were symptoms of his unhappiness.

Photography became an escape. Roald was permitted to make a small darkroom for himself in an unused corner of one of the classroom buildings. Here he could have the privacy that was otherwise non-existent in a boarding school. He learned to develop his own pictures, use special lighting effects, enlarge and mount his photographs for exhibits. It was a serious hobby, and Roald was very talented. He won prizes from the Royal Photographic Society in London and from the Photographic Society of Holland.

Cadbury's Chocolates were produced in a factory near Repton School. The company used to send boxes of their latest creations to the school for the boys to taste and comment on. As he nibbled on chocolate bars, Roald would imagine the factory looking like a laboratory, where white-coated workers experimented with new flavors, and pots of chocolate bubbled away on stoves. *Charlie and the Chocolate Factory,* one of the most popular children's books of all time, grew from this fantasy.

Roald was happy when it was time to leave Repton. He was ready to get out and see the world. Roald applied for a job with the Shell Oil Company, and in 1934, at the age of eighteen, was hired. After two years of training in London, his wish for travel was granted. He was sent to East Africa, to spend three years at Shell's facility in Dar es Salaam, Tanganyika (now Tanzania).

"I was off to the land of palm trees and coconuts and coral reefs and lions and elephants and deadly snakes, and a white hunter....told me that if a black mamba bit you, you died within the hour writhing in agony and foaming at the mouth. I couldn't wait."

Roald's African adventure was as exciting as he had hoped it would be. He saved a servant from the attack of a black mamba. He sold his first piece of writing to a newspaper—an eye-witness account of a woman who was carried off by a lion and saved herself by playing dead until the lion wandered away.

In 1939, England declared war on Germany. Roald, still in Africa, went to Nairobi, Kenya to join the Royal Air Force. At six feet, six inches tall, it was a tight squeeze for him to fit into the cockpit of an airplane—especially when he had to sit on his six-inch-thick parachute. Roald was so tall his head stuck up above the windshield. The force of the wind in his face made it necessary for him to duck his head down into the cockpit every few seconds in order to breathe. He soon learned that a scarf wrapped over his mouth and nose helped.

Roald enjoyed his training flights. He flew over herds of buffalo and wildebeest, gazelles and giraffes. He saw rhino, elephants, lions, and leopards. After six months he was sent to Iraq to complete his training. He was then ordered to the western desert of Libya to fight the Italians.

Roald was told where he would find his new squadron. Unfortunately, the officer who gave him his flight instructions was either misinformed or careless. He misdirected Roald by several hundred miles. Flying low, searching for his destination, Roald began to run low on fuel. Seeking desperately for a safe place to bring his plane down, Roald ran out of time. The plane crashed and burst into flames. Suffering a skull fracture, his nose broken and pushed into his face, Roald managed to drag himself free of his burning plane. Fortunately a unit of British soldiers who had seen his plane go down arrived to rescue him.

It was six months before Roald recovered and was fit to fly again. In April, 1941, he set off once more to join his squadron, now in Greece. For two months Roald fought the Germans over Greece, engaging in aerial battles called dogfights and by some luck surviving when many of his comrades were shot down. It soon became apparent, however, that he had not completely recovered from his crash injuries. Suffering from severe head pains, Roald was declared medically unfit for combat service and was sent back to England.

After a brief visit with his mother and sisters, Roald was assigned to the British Embassy in Washington, D. C. as an assistant air attache. The U.S. had not yet entered the war and his real job was to be a spy. He was instructed to seek out any information that might affect the British war effort and report it to the British Secret Intelligence Service.

Tall and handsome, Roald could be very charming. He got himself invited to official functions and social events, listened to all the rumors about Washington attitudes toward the war and post-war reconstruction, and reported his findings to the British foreign ministry.

Although he discovered nothing his government didn't already know, Roald relished his role. He had learned to distrust authority during his schooldays, and he had observed the incompetence of many military leaders while with the RAF. Being a spy fit right in with his inherent distrust of rules and the conventions of society.

The United States entered World War II in December, 1941. In order to promote enthusiasm among Americans for the war effort, the British government sent C. S. Forester, a well-known author of adventure novels, to Washington. Forester's job was to write articles extolling the heroic feats of the Allied Forces, and place them in popular American magazines. Roald Dahl, the ex-RAF pilot now serving his country in Washington, was a perfect subject. Forester asked Roald to meet him at a restaurant for an interview about his plane crash. As they talked, their food grew cold. Roald suggested they concentrate on their meal. He would jot down some notes about the crash and send them to Forester later for his article.

What C. S. Forester received from Roald was more than just some notes. Roald sent him a complete, well-written account which required no rewriting at all. Forester informed Roald he was instructing his agent to place the article as written.

The success of this article encouraged Roald to try his hand at writing short stories. During his remaining time in Washington, he wrote several fictionalized accounts about flying in wartime and submitted them to prominent magazines. Not one of them was rejected. It was enough to make Roald reconsider his entire plan for the future. He decided that when he returned to England after the war he would quit Shell Oil and become a full-time writer.

The short stories were written for an adult audience, but Roald had an idea for a children's book, too. RAF pilots had a long-standing joke about gremlins—little creatures who are responsible for anything that malfunctions in a fighter plane. In 1942, Roald wrote a children's novel, *The Gremlins,* based on the RAF fable. *The Gremlins* (a Royal Air Force Story by Flight Lieutenant Roald Dahl) was published by Walt Disney as a picture book in 1943.

Roald did not plan to write only for children. He returned to England after the war intending to write stories for adults. He settled in with his mother outside a village called Great Missenden. They had a farm with dogs, ducks, a cow, a goat, ferrets, canaries, and parrots. Roald began to write. He worked hard at his craft, and by the late 1940's was a leading short story writer, selling two or three stories every year to prestigious magazines. His stories had vivid details, carefully constructed plots, and surprise endings. In 1946, Roald's first book for adults was published. *Over to You* was a collection of stories, including most of his war stories. Critics, as well as the public, were enthusiastic about the book.

Roald's stories were selling well in America, but he was not having much luck placing them in British magazines. In 1951, Roald decided to apply for a permanent American visa. He moved to New York City, living in the house of a friend who was out of the country at the time. It was in New York that friends introduced Roald to a movie and stage actress, Patricia Neal.

Roald and Pat were soon a couple, and in July 1953, they married. They rented an apartment in New York City where they spent part of each year. Their summers were spent in Great Missenden, where they bought a home named "Gipsy House." There was an old garden shed in the yard which Roald converted into a writing studio. Here he worked daily, following a rigid schedule. He wrote from 10:00 A. M. until noon, and from 4:00 P. M. to 6:00 P. M., seven days a week.

In 1954, Roald published a second collection of short stories, *Someone Like You*. These were bizarre tales, full of dark humor. The book was very successful, winning the Mystery Writers of America Edgar Allan Poe Award. Critics were beginning to comment unfavorably on Roald's work, however. Although there was agreement about his skill, many reviewers felt there was too much heartlessness and distortion in his tales. Roald began to have trouble selling stories to magazines. To make up for the lost income, Roald turned to writing for the movies. He worked on the film version of *Moby Dick*.

In the spring of 1955, Pat and Roald's first child, Olivia, was born. Roald doted on her. A nurse was hired to take care of the baby while her parents worked, but Roald spent as much time as he could with her. The Dahl's second daughter, Tessa, was born in 1957, and in

1960, they had a son, Theo. Roald was a caring, attentive father, playing with the children much of the day, and telling them wonderful stories.

Although stories for the children seemed to come to him easily, Roald was having difficulty finding new ideas for his adult stories. He decided to turn some of the tales with which he had entertained Olivia and Tessa into full-length children's novels. *James and the Giant Peach* was his first effort. As soon as it was sent off to his publisher, he started working on *Charlie and the Chocolate Factory.*

When Theo was four months old, he was struck by a car while being wheeled across a New York City street in his baby buggy. His head injuries were severe and resulted in a continuing build-up of fluid inside his skull. The treatment for this was the insertion of a tube with a one-way valve which drained the fluid away from the brain. Frequent clogging of the valve meant the baby had to undergo repeated operations so the tube could be cleared. Theo had frightening setbacks and required constant nursing and hospitalization. The Dahls decided to return to England where medical treatment would be free and there would be relatives nearby to help out.

Roald was very concerned by the inefficiency of the valve in Theo's drainage tube. He was sure there must be a better method. When he met a hydraulic engineer while on an outing with his daughters, he mentioned the problem to him. Soon the two of them were meeting to discuss possible solutions. Stanley Wade, the engineer, designed an improved valve, and he and Roald showed it to Kenneth Till, the neurologist who was treating Theo. Till suggested some refinements, and in 1962, the Wade-Dahl-Till valve was patented. By this time Theo's condition had improved. He no longer needed the new valve, but it was very successful in the treatment of other children with similar injuries, and was exported all over the world.

In the fall of 1962, tragedy again struck the Dahl family. Measles vaccinations were not yet routine in England, and Olivia caught the disease. It was an unusually severe case. She developed an extremely high fever, went into a coma, and died shortly after. Roald was devastated. He brooded, withdrew from friends and family, and was unable to write.

Roald's depression and writing slump lasted nearly a year. He finally began to regain his spirits when he learned that Pat was expecting another child. Ophelia was born in May, 1964. Roald finally completed *Charlie and the Chocolate Factory,* which had been put off while he dealt with his personal problems. Roald's editor was doubtful about the book's chances. He felt that some of the humor was in bad taste. Roald agreed with him, but argued that children find bad taste funny. The book was a great success.

Whenever Pat was on location making a movie the whole family traveled with her. In February of 1965, she was working on a movie in California. She was pregnant again, expecting her fifth child in the summer. Suddenly one morning, she felt severe pain in her head. Roald took no chances. He called an ambulance immediately. Pat had suffered a massive stroke. The doctors told Roald his quick action had saved her life.

Pat underwent surgery to remove the blood clots from her brain, but much damage had been done. She couldn't talk, and she was paralyzed on her right side. Her speech came back gradually, but her words were often gibberish. She couldn't name everyday objects, and her partial paralysis made her words unclear.

Roald had three goals. He wanted the baby to be born safely. He wanted Pat to recover and return to work. He wanted to become so rich that money would never be a problem again. Eventually, all three goals were achieved.

Lucy, Pat and Roald's last child, was born in August, 1965. Roald helped Pat regain her speech and her coordination, often urging her to continue her exercises when she was exhausted. After five years, she finally returned to her movie career. Now Roald could concentrate on his writing again.

During Pat's recovery, Roald had worked on two movie scripts—the James Bond film, *You Only Live Twice,* and the screen adaptation of another Ian Fleming book, *Chitty Chitty Bang Bang.* In 1970, he wrote the screenplay for *Charlie and the Chocolate Factory* which was filmed as *Willie Wonka and the Chocolate Factory.*

Several magazines reprinted his short stories, and he sold film rights for others. His collections of short stories were printed in paperback, and gained a new audience. Roald began to receive a substantial regular income from the royalties on all these projects.

Roald's problems were not over, however. He and Pat were having marital problems. They tried to hold the family together for several years in spite of their growing differences, but in 1983 they divorced. Pat returned to America and Roald and the children remained at Gipsy House.

Roald married again. His second wife, Felicity Crosland, was an interior decorator who soon turned Gipsy House into the kind of home Roald had always dreamed of. Together, he and Felicity pursued Roald's long-standing interests in art, antiques, wine, and cooking.

They entertained frequently, and wrote a cookbook together which included their favorite recipes.

From 1980 until his death from leukemia on November 23, 1990, Roald published a book nearly every year. His fame grew with each book, although he has never been free from criticism.His books have been called vulgar, violent, and disrespectful to adults. On the other hand, many reviewers have praised the high literary quality of his work. *The Witches* received England's prestigious Whitbread Award. In 1984, the "Deutscher Jugendliteraturpreis"—the major German prize for children's books—was awarded to *The BFG.* A report by the Book Marketing Council in the 1980's showed that of the ten best sellers in children's books at the time, four—*The BFG, George's Marvelous Medicine, Revolting Rhymes,* and *The Twits*—were by Roald Dahl.

Roald was not very concerned with what critics said about his work. What was important to him was his undeniable popularity with the children for whom he wrote."If my books can help children become readers, then I feel I have accomplished something important."

Notes:

Page 29   "Great excitement..." Roald Dahl, *Boy: Tales of Childhood* (Farrar, Straus and Giroux, Inc., 1984), p. 124.

Page 31   "like an undertaker's apprentice..." Dahl, *Boy,* p. 126.

Page 32   "I was off..." Dahl, *Boy,* p. 159.

Page 40   "If my books..." Mark West, "Interview with Roald Dahl", *Children's Literature in Education* (June 21, 1990), p. 66.

For further reading about Roald Dahl:

Dahl, Roald. Boy: *Tales of Childhood.* New York: Farrar, Straus and Giroux, 1984.

___. *Going Solo.* England: Penguin Books, 1986.

Treglown, Jeremy. *Roald Dahl: a Biography.* New York: Farrar, Straus and Giroux, 1994.

Warren, Alan. *Roald Dahl.* San Bernardino: The Borgo Press, 1988.

West, Mark I. *Roald Dahl.* New York: Twayne Publishers, 1992

Books for Young Readers
by Roald Dahl

1943 The Gremlins

1961 James and the Giant Peach

1964 Charlie and the Chocolate Factory

1966 The Magic Finger

1970 Fantastic Mr. Fox

1972 Charlie and the Great Glass Elevator

1975 Danny: The Champion of the World

1976 The Enormous Crocodile

1977 The Wonderful Story of Henry Sugar and Six More

1980 The Twits

1981 George's Marvelous Medicine

1982 The BFG

1983 The Witches

1985 The Giraffe and the Pelly and Me

1988 Matilda

1990 Esio Trot

1991 The Minpins

MADELEINE L'ENGLE
Lighting a Candle to See By

Twelve-year-old Madeleine Camp smiled proudly. The prize winners in the school poetry contest had just been announced, and her poem had won! Her excitement soon turned to humiliation, however. Her homeroom teacher said, "Madeleine couldn't possibly have written that poem. She must have copied it from somewhere. She's not very bright, you know."

Madeleine L'Engle Camp was born November 29, 1918. She was named after her mother, an accomplished pianist. Madeleine's father, Charles, was the drama and music critic for the *New York Herald-Evening Sun*. Her father's lungs had been damaged by mustard gas in World War I. Not long after Madeleine's birth, poor health forced her father to give up his job as a reporter and turn to writing short stories, plays, and movies. Mrs. Camp had health problems, too. She was considered "frail" and sometimes spent weeks in bed while a uniformed nurse managed the household.

Madeleine's parents had been married for twenty years before she was born. They had a wide circle of friends who were artists, writers, and musicians. When they were feeling well, the Camps gave frequent parties in their apartment near Central Park in New York City. When they weren't entertaining, they usually went out each evening to dinner or to a concert.

Although Madeleine was a loved and wanted child, her parents were not prepared to alter their lifestyle for the needs of a baby. They decided to hire someone to take charge of their daughter's upbringing. Mrs. Camp wanted Madeleine to learn to be graceful and confident. She thought a dancer or circus performer should be hired to teach Madeleine and take care of her. Mr. Camp disagreed. He wanted his daughter to be raised like an upper-class English child, with meals on a tray in the nursery, dancing and piano lessons, and a nanny to supervise her childhood.

Madeleine's nanny was a kind and loving woman who did her best to provide a secure and happy environment. Madeleine took her meals alone at a small table, usually with a book propped in front of her. She did not mind—she loved to be left alone to read and daydream. At noon on Sundays she dined with her parents, but these were awkward occasions. Madeleine's parents had little in common with their small child, and not much to say to her.

Although Madeleine was alone much of the time as a child, she was not lonely. Her mother and her nanny both read to her daily, and Madeleine wrote her own stories as well. At the age of five she wrote and illustrated her first story. From then on, she knew she would one day be a writer.

At age six Madeleine was enrolled in a small private school. She was a good reader and enjoyed the school. When it came time to enter the fourth grade Madeleine was sent her to another private school, she was very unhappy. The new school stressed sports. Madeleine limped as a result of a childhood illness which had left one leg shorter than the other. When teams were chosen in the schoolyard, Madeleine was the last one selected, and her teammates would groan when her name was called.

Not only did Madeleine feel disliked by the students, she also felt disliked by the teachers. Her intense shyness made her seem like a slow learner. Sometimes the teachers even showed her papers to the class as examples of poor work. Madeleine learned to think of herself as clumsy, ugly, dumb, and unpopular. She longed to be left alone with a book. Although Madeleine was miserable, her father would not let her change schools. Her mother had made the decision to send her there, and Mr. Camp insisted Madeleine abide by her choice.

At home Madeline shared her mother's constant worry about her father's poor health. She also endured two attacks of iritis—an inflammation of the iris of the eye—that year. Her doctor warned that a third incident would probably cause her to lose her sight. For the rest of her life, Madeleine was afraid that she would someday become blind. She eased her fears and unhappiness by writing. "My real life was not in school, but in my stories and my dreams," she wrote later.

Every day she wrote glorious adventures starring the girl she wanted to be. Because her schoolwork never met with her teachers' approval, Madeleine wrote her stories instead of doing her homework. She never took the stories to school. Her teachers had no idea that she wrote so much. When Madeleine was accused of copying the poem which won the school contest during her sixth grade year, her angry mother gathered up armfuls of Madeleine's stories and took them to school to demonstrate her daughter's writing ability. The school authorities agreed that she could have written the poem after all. Madeleine never forgot how ashamed and frustrated she felt to have been so misjudged.

The next fall, Madeleine was sent to yet another private school. But this time Madeleine's intelligence was appreciated by her teachers. Her papers were shown to the class as an example of good work. Her writing was encouraged and she was assigned more difficult books to challenge her.

Madeleine loved her new school and began to regain her self-confidence. Unfortunately, she was able to spend only one year there. Mr. Camp suffered increasingly from his weak lungs, and was subject to frequent bouts of pneumonia. On the advice of his doctor, the family moved to France in 1930, seeking the clean, dry air of the French Alps.

Madeleine was sent to a boarding school in Switzerland. It was a terrible experience. The school was very strict. Every hour of Madeleine's day was regimented. Madeleine coped by creating an inner world for herself. She recorded what she saw, felt, and did in a diary. She turned to favorite books for comfort. She loved *The Bastables*, by E. Nesbit and *The Secret Garden,* by Frances Hodgson Burnett. The books of George MacDonald—*The Princess and the Goblin* and *The Princess and Curdie*—also had a great impact on her. But her very favorite was *Emily of New Moon*, by L. M. Montgomery, which seemed to Madeleine to have been written just for her. She reread it at least once a month for two years.

Madeleine learned the useful technique of blocking out distractions in order to concentrate. She had no privacy for her writing, so she learned to close her ears to the voices of teachers and other students as she wrote poems during her classes and study periods.

In 1932, the family moved again. This time they went to Florida, where Madeleine's grandmother was very ill. They lived in a house by the ocean. One of Madeleine's greatest pleasures was to walk along the beach with her father and recite her poems to him. Sometimes he would respond with just a nod, but when he thought one of the poems was especially good, he would delight her with his praise.

In the fall Madeleine entered Ashley Hall Boarding School in Charleston, South Carolina. Here at last she was happy and popular. She took part in the school's many activities, becoming a leader in clubs, acting in school plays, and serving as president of the student council during her senior year.

Many of Madeleine's poems were published in the school's literary magazine. In her senior year she edited the magazine, and received further recognition for her writing ability when one of her poems won a school prize.

The accomplishments of Madeleine's senior year at Ashley Hall were overshadowed by her father's death from pneumonia in the fall. It was a blow to Madeleine. She grew closer to her mother after her father's death, and shared her writing with her. Up until this time, Madeleine had written mostly fairy tales with herself as the heroine. Now she began to write more realistic stories, using incidents from her own and her parents' lives. Madeleine's mother saw her talent and encouraged her writing.

Madeleine applied for admission to Smith College in Massachusetts. She thought she had not done well enough on the college entrance tests, and was surprised when the school accepted her. Majoring in English, Madeleine enjoyed her studies. Her experience with the literary magazine in high school led her to start a similar publication at Smith. She continued to write both stories and poems, and was the recipient of the college's Elizabeth Babcock Poetry Prize, winning $2,500.

Madeleine also wrote plays at Smith, some of which were performed by her fellow students. She grew to love acting and the theater. When she graduated with honors in 1941, Madeleine still knew she wanted to be a writer, but she also knew that establishing a writing career takes time. In the meantime, she needed to find a job.

Madeleine moved to New York City, where she rented an apartment with three college friends, and began to look for an acting job. She managed to get a small part in a play, plus an understudy role. This meant she had to learn the roles of other actors and be ready to step into their parts if they were unable to go on. Madeleine's salary for this first job was $65.00 a week.

Madeleine loved New York City. Not only was it her birthplace, it had music, art, and theater to offer. It was also the publishing center of the country. She knew it was where she belonged.

When her roommates discussed how to divide housekeeping chores, Madeleine announced she would do the cooking. She learned by doing, experimenting with tastes and textures. Her childhood experience with French cooking inspired her and she became accomplished at creating new dishes.

Madeleine immersed herself in theater. She saw every play she could, often earning standing-room tickets by selling war bonds in the theater lobbies before performances. She spent her days at rehearsals and her evenings at shows, then went home to the bustle of three roommates. Madeleine had no quiet time or place in which to write. She needed her own apartment.

In the summer of 1942, Madeleine moved to a small apartment in the Greenwich Village section of New York. She soon began sending stories to magazines. It was important to Madeleine that her work be judged on its own merits and not be accepted just because the publishers knew her father. She decided to drop her last name. She became Madeleine L'Engle.

Madeleine sold short stories to literary magazines. This brought her some prestige, but little money. Then a publisher contacted her. He had seen her stories and wondered whether she was writing a novel. Madeleine had been working for some time on a novel based on her boarding school experiences. She sent it to the publisher, who assigned a good editor to work with her. The novel, *The Small Rain*, was rewritten and refined until it was ready to publish.

Madeleine's first book had good reviews and excellent sales, but she still needed her acting job to make ends meet. As soon as *The Small Rain* was published, Madeleine began a role as a walk-on in a production of *The Cherry Orchard*. The leading man in the play was a young actor named Hugh Franklin. Madeleine and Hugh were soon dating regularly, and in January, 1946, they married.

The first years of their marriage were eventful. Madeleine's second book, *Ilsa*, was published in 1946. They bought and renovated an old farmhouse in Connecticut they named *Crosswicks*. In 1947, their first child, Josephine, was born. Hugh's acting career meant they kept unusual hours. Madeleine would put the baby to bed early and then wake her up when Hugh returned home from the theater. They would play with Josephine until 2:00 A. M., when they all went to bed.

For the next three years, Madeleine and Hugh spent winters in New York and summers at *Crosswicks*. Hugh was away much of the time as his career took him on the road. He toured with plays and also landed television roles. Because she did not own a TV set, Madeleine would take Josephine with her to a neighborhood bar where she would watch Hugh's television programs.

Madeleine and Hugh wanted another child, but they were concerned because neither had a stable job and Hugh was often away. They decided that Hugh would give up his acting career and look for a job near *Crosswicks*. They found a general store that was for sale and bought it. In spite of their lack of experience, they were soon earning a steady income from the store and from the four books Madeleine had published.

The Franklin's son, Bion, was born in 1952. Now Madeleine was looking after two children, and was helping in the store part-time. She taught Sunday school and directed the church choir. To save money she canned fruits and vegetables. In 1956, Madeleine and Hugh took in Maria, the seven-year-old daughter of close friends who had died. A year later they adopted her.

This was Madeleine's first experience as a member of a community and she enjoyed her neighbors, but life was becoming hectic. With family responsibilities, housework in a cold and drafty farmhouse, frequent guests, and several pets, Madeleine had trouble finding writing time. She grew frustrated. She needed uninterrupted time to write. After thinking about her problem, she told her family what her new schedule would be. She would write at night after the children were in bed. In the morning she would sleep late, and Hugh would be responsible for making breakfast.

Madeleine kept writing and sending manuscripts to publishers. Even though very little of her work sold between 1952 and 1959, she didn't give up. She would feel less discouraged, she knew, if she had other writers nearby to talk to. Also, she missed the theater, music, and art she had enjoyed in New York City. Hugh agreed. They decided to sell the store and return to New York for the winters, where Hugh would resume his acting career.

Before settling into city life, the Franklins decided to take a camping trip. During this trip, an idea came to Madeleine. She thought of three names—Mrs. Who, Mrs. Whatsit, and Mrs. Which. She didn't have an idea for a story yet, but she knew those three characters would be important. She began work on another novel.

By the end of 1959, Madeleine had finished *A Wrinkle In Time.* Mrs. Who, Mrs. Whatsit, and Mrs. Which were in it, and so was *Crosswicks.* This book was different from her first six books, but she was pleased with it. She had written it out of her faith in God, and she knew it was good.

One by one, publishers rejected the book, saying it talked too much about evil. It was very discouraging, and she was ready to tell her agent to give up. Then a friend of her mother's suggested she take the manuscript to John Farrar, of Farrar, Straus and Giroux. Because Madeleine's friend knew Mr. Farrar, Madeleine was able to get an appointment with him directly instead of submitting the book to a reader. Farrar loved her book. He agreed that it was unusual and might not be successful, but he wanted to publish it anyway.

Published in 1962, *A Wrinkle In Time* surprised Madeleine by becoming an immediate success. The next year she was surprised again when the book won the Newbery Medal, one of the most prestigious awards in children's literature. *A Wrinkle In Time* also won the American Library Association's Notable Book Award, the Lewis Carroll Shelf Award, the Sequoyah Award, and was a runner-up for the Hans Christian Andersen Award. It made Madeleine a "literary star."

This experience taught Madeleine to trust her own judgment about her books and to be patient and persistent when publishers rejected her work, even though it hurt. She decided to write about ideas that were important to her. Publishing was a way to share her ideas with others.

Madeleine's writing career seemed to be back on track after nearly a decade of disappointing rejections. She wrote steadily, daily. Writing was something she needed to do. Her children noticed that she got cranky if something kept her away from her typewriter.

Madeleine wrote more books about the O'Keefe family featured in *A Wrinkle in Time,* as well as several about the Austin family. She used *Crosswicks* as the setting for many of the books. The events of her fiction are often based on her family life, but she denies that her children were the models for the characters. "I would not presume to write out of my children. My protagonists, male and female, are me."

Madeleine continued to write while her children grew up, married, and had children of their own. She also spoke at schools, libraries, and colleges, even while enduring a flare-up of her old eye problem—iritis—this time coupled with glaucoma. The terrible pain and the fear of blindness placed demands on her courage.

In 1985, Madeleine and Hugh were invited to travel to Egypt as unofficial goodwill ambassadors for the United States Information Agency. There she gave readings and spoke about her work. The next year they were asked to tour China.

After the successful China trip, on which they were very happy together, they learned that Hugh was suffering from cancer. Hugh's illness and eventual death in September, 1986, was devastating to Madeleine. Again summoning her great reserves of courage, she began a new book. *Two-Part Invention* is the story of their relationship. Writing it helped Madeleine heal.

Madeleine now lives part of the year in her New York City apartment with two of her grandchildren. She still spends summers at *Crosswicks*. She has continued her childhool habit of keeping a journal, and finds them helpful in her research. When she needs to know how a thirteen-year-old thinks, she can look up her own thoughts at that age.

Madeleine teaches writing classes at the private school her children attended. She travels to teach and give talks and answers letters from her readers. Mostly, though, she writes.

Madeleine's faith in God has always been an important influence in her writing. She is concerned about children who are not taught religious faith. She is very active in her own church, and when her children were growing up she persuaded the congregation to open the church's door to after-school activities to get children inside the building. Many of her books grow out of her interest in astrophysics, the study of physics and space. She combines this challenge to the imagination with her ideas about the nature of God and the meaning of the universe.

Madeleine firmly believes in the moral consequences of the writer's work. "Like it or not, we either add to the darkness of indifference and out and out evil which surrounds us or we light a candle to see by."

Notes:

Page 45   "Madeleine couldn't possibly..." Donald R. Gallo, ed.,
            Speaking for Ourselves (Urbana, IL: National Council
            of Teachers of English, 1990), p. 116.

Page 47   "My real life..." Doreen Gonzales, *Madeleine L'Engle:
            Author of A Wrinkle In Time* (New York: Dillon Press,
            1991), p. 24.

Page 54   "I would not presume..." Madeleine L'Engle, *The Irra-
            tional Season* (New York: Farrar, Straus and Giroux,
            1977), p. 16.

Page 56   "Like it or not..." Madeleine L'Engle, *A Circle of Quiet*
            (New York: Farrar, Straus and Giroux, 1971), p. 99.

For further reading aboaut
Madeleine L'Engle:

Gallo, Donald R. *Speaking for Ourselves.* Urbana, IL: National
Council of Teachers of English, 1990

Gonzales, Doreen. *Madeleine L'Engle: Author of A Wrinkle In Time.*
New York: Dillon Press, 1991.

Hettinga, Donald R. *Presenting Madeleine L'Engle.* New York:
Twayne Publishers, 1993.

L'Engle, Madeleine. *A Circle of Quiet.* New York: Farrar, Straus and
Giroux, 1971.

___. *The Irrational Season.* New York: Farrar, Straus and Giroux,
1977.

___. *Two-Part Invention: The Story of a Marriage.* New York:
Farrar, Straus and Giroux, 1988.

Yancy, Philip, ed. "George MacDonald: Nourishment for a Private
World." *In Reality and the Vision: Eighteen Contemporary
Writers Tell Who They Read and Why.* Dallas: Word, 1990:
111-121.

Books for Young Readers
by Madeleine L'Engle

1945	The Small Rain	1973	A Wind in the Door
1946	Ilsa	1976	Dragons in the Water
1949	And Both Were Young	1978	A Swiftly Tilting Planet
1951	Camilla Dickinson	1980	A Ring of Endless Light
1957	A Winter's Love	1981	The Anti-Muffins
1960	Meet the Austins	1982	The Sphinx at Dawn
1962	A Wrinkle in Time	1984	A House Like a Lotus
1963	The Moon by Night	1986	Many Waters
1964	The Twenty-Four Days before Christmas	1987	A Cry Like a Bell
		1988	Ladder of Angels
1965	The Arm of the Starfish	1989	An Acceptable Time
1968	The Young Unicorns	1990	The Glorious Impossible
1969	Dance in the Desert	1994	Troubling a Star
1970	Intergalactic P. S. 3		

Betsy Byars

Betsy was excited. Her father had just brought home some remnants of cloth from the cotton mill where he had a position as an executive. Betsy, a second grader, planned to make herself a new skirt. She loved to be busy. Because her father frequently brought free material home she had been sewing since she was very young. This time, maybe she could make something her mother would allow her to wear out of the yard.

"I sewed fast, without patterns, and with great hope and determination, and that is approximately the same way that I write."

Betsy Cromer was born in Charlotte, North Carolina on August 7, 1928. Her father, George, was a civil engineer by training. Her mother, Nan, was a homemaker.

Betsy's earliest memory is of her father reading her *Goldilocks and the Three Bears*. She learned to read at a very young age, and thinks that it was her older sister, Nancy, who taught her.

The Cromer's spent part of their time in the city of Charlotte, and part of their time in the country where the cotton mill was located. There the children had pet rabbits and a goat named Buttsy to pull Betsy in a little cart.

Betsy's love of animals led to her first career goal. She would work in a zoo, where she would take care of orphaned baby animals. With her best friend, Louise, Betsy spent many hours playing "zoo." The goats and rabbits would be penned up. Other animals would be collected for exhibit—cats, turtles, lots of insects. The featured exhibit was always the leech collection. Betsy and Louise would wade in a small pond near Betsy's house. When they came out of the water, leeches would be fastened to their legs. If they worked quickly, they could pull the leeches off before they became firmly attached. If they were too slow, the leeches would have to be pried off with a stick—a painful process.

Betsy was eager to start school. She had long envied her sister's glowing reports of the first grade teacher who introduced the class to exciting activities and wonderful books. Betsy couldn't wait to have Miss Harriet for her teacher. When she arrived at school the first day, she was taken to the auditorium where she learned there were three first grade teachers. The children's names were called by class, and they were told to line up behind their teacher. When Miss Harriet's list of students was called, Betsy's name was not among them. Betsy had waited three years to be in her class, and she wasn't going to be disappointed. She lined up behind Miss Harriet anyway, and marched to her classroom with the others. When the principal came to take her to her assigned class, Betsy looked down at the floor and shook her head. Miss Harriet was sympathetic, and asked the principal to let her stay. Betsy's determination was rewarded. She loved everything about first grade.

Betsy's childhood was full of adventures. She once touched a mummy on a dare at the science museum in Charlotte. The boy who dared her, Louisa's older brother, Bubba, then frightened her by telling her that her hand would become a "mummy hand," that would turn everything she touched into a mummy. She was pretty sure she didn't believe him, but went home and scrubbed her hand anyway.

Betsy may have been one of the first children to ride on a skateboard. The neighborhood gang nailed half a roller skate to the front end of a piece of wood, and the other half to the rear. They decided Betsy, the youngest, should be the first to try it out. There was a steep hill nearby, down which they had been warned not to ride their bikes or skates. Nothing had been said about skateboards, however, so this was the site they chose for Betsy's test run. Since this was the first time they had ever tried a skateboard, no one knew that it should be done standing up. Betsy sat on the board, the others gave it a push, and she started careening down the hill. Fortunately, the back wheels came off almost immediately and the board came to a halt before she was seriously injured.

When she was a child Betsy had no plans to become a writer. No teacher ever suggested the possibility either. She did have a teacher in third grade who gave her and the rest of the class an important bit of writing advice. "Write about what you know." At the time, it seemed to Betsy to be poor advice. What did a girl from rural North Carolina know worth writing about? It wasn't until many years later that she understood how important this rule was. "...one of the best gifts a writer can give a reader is the feeling 'this writer knows what she's talking about.'"

Betsy did a lot of reading as a child—everything from *Uncle Wiggly* to the *National Geographic*. She read *The Bobbsey Twins* and the humorous adventures of a group of boy detectives written by Leo Edwards.

By the time Betsy started high school she had two major goals—having fun, and studying just enough to keep her father happy. She flirted with boys in the halls at school and talked about the latest movie stars with friends. She wore the current high school uniform—dirty saddle shoes, angora socks, pleated skirts, enormous sweaters, and pearls. "The important thing was to look exactly like everybody else," she remembers.

Betsy didn't take her school subjects very seriously, but her father did. To please him she made sure her grades never fell below a B. When her father, a civil engineer, urged her to major in math in college, Betsy decided she might as well agree. "The only thing I really loved to do was read and I knew I couldn't get a job doing that."

Betsy entered Furman University in Greenville, South Carolina in 1947. She did well in her math courses at first, especially when the work involved word problems; but the courses were more difficult her second year. Finally, calculus defeated her. She told her father she was changing her major to English. She also changed schools, spending her last two years at Queens College in Charlotte. In 1950 she received her Bachelor of Arts degree. Three weeks after graduation, on June 24, 1950, she married Edward Ford Byars.

Ed was a graduate student in engineering at Clemson University in South Carolina. The Byars spent the next six years at Clemson while Ed finished his degree. He then accepted a position on the faculty. The couple had many friends among the graduate students and young faculty members, and Betsy was busy caring for her daughter Laurie, who was born in 1951, and Betsy Ann, who came along in 1953. Three years later Betsy was pregnant again.

Ed decided to go back to graduate school, this time at the University of Illinois, in Urbana. They moved into a small apartment in a student housing complex. Betsy was not happy here. Most of the women in the complex were students or had jobs outside the home. With no friends, and with Ed busy all day and most evenings with his studies, Betsy was bored. She had often wondered whether she could write for magazines, and this seemed like the time to try it.

Betsy bought copies of several popular magazines to study the kinds of articles they published. There she bought an old used typewriter and set to work. She was elated when she sold her first article to the *Saturday Evening Post.* She felt certain she was on her way to a successful writing career.

Writing careers are not easy to establish, however, and she did not sell another article for seven months. Gradually her sales became more regular, and her humorous pieces were published in magazines like *Look, Everywoman's Magazine,* and *TV Guide.*

She also wrote some stories for children, but had no luck finding a publisher for them. In the meantime, the family grew. She had another daughter, Nan, in 1956, and a son, Guy, in 1958. After finishing his doctorate, Ed was offered a position on the faculty of the University of West Virginia, and the family moved again.

The hills surrounding Morgantown, West Virginia, were beautiful, and Betsy decided to use this setting for a novel. The independent attitude of the people there gave her ideas for characters and story plots. Betsy sold her first children's book, *Clementine*, in 1962. The reviews were not very good, and her next book, *The Dancing Camel*, did not do well either. Still, she kept writing. Two more books followed in 1966 and 1967. Then Betsy took a course in children's literature at the university. She was introduced to the type of book known as realistic fiction. This gave her new ideas for subject matter that was better suited to her writing style.

The next two books she worked on, *Trouble River* and *The Midnight Fox*, were successes. Both were named Child Study Association of America Books of the Year, and *Trouble River* was designated a Notable Book for 1969 by the American Library Association. The personalities and many of the activities of Betsy's own children went into *The Midnight Fox*. She and her children always communicated well. They told her what they were doing and things that happened in school. They were a great source of story ideas during these years.

Still unsure of her future as a writer, Betsy decided to enroll at the University of West Virginia and take courses for a degree in Special Education. Tutoring mentally handicapped children was part of her course work, and this gave her some insight into the problems and personalities of these children. The idea for *The Summer of the Swans* grew from this experience. This book was Betsy's big breakthrough. It won the Newbery Medal and was named a Junior Literary Club book, Horn Book honor book, and American Library Association Notable Book. Its overwhelming success gave her increased confidence in her writing ability. She dropped out of graduate school and became a full-time writer.

In the 1970's, following the success of her Newbery book, Betsy published a new book every year. The books were well-reviewed and very popular with young readers, but she received no major critical awards. Then, *The Pinballs,* which was published in 1977, won two awards which were very important to Betsy. This story of three foster children trying to come to grips with the problems of their lives received high praise from critics and readers alike. It was awarded the California Young Readers Medal and the Georgia Children's Book Award. Both of these honors are voted on by fourth through seventh grade children.

In 1980, Betsy once again won major critical awards—this time for *The Night Swimmers.* This novel received the American Book Award and was named a Boston Globe—Horn Book Honor Book. Since that time nearly every book she has written has been an award winner—an indication of her skillful touch in portraying the real problems children struggle with.

In 1980, after twenty years in West Virginia, the Byars family moved to South Carolina. They bought a townhouse where she worked upstairs next to window looking out on a lake. Betsy wondered whether she'd be able to write anymore without her huge desk by the window looking out on the West Virginia hills. Before long she found that the scenery surrounding her new home inspired good stories, too. Betsy continued to turn out award-winning books, now with a little South Carolina flavor to them.

When Betsy plans to write a book about something, she first goes to the library and reads every book she can find about that subject. "For me, reading books and writing them are tied together. The words of other writers teach me and refresh me and inspire me."

If she is going to use an unusual setting for the book, she visits the setting and absorbs the atmosphere while taking notes on all her observations. When she decided to write a book about a girl and her grandfather who fly across the United States in a small airplane, she researched the book by flying across the country with Ed in a two-seater J-3 Piper Cub. They flew for seven days, eight hours per day. Betsy knew "journey books" like this are easy to write. Very little plot construction is required—the book is really just a series of interesting events. She wrote the book, but no publisher would take it. "Not enough plot construction," they said. Betsy has rewritten the book about seventeen times so far, but still has not sold it.

Betsy has done other unusual or difficult things because she thought the experience might someday become part of a book. She went on Space Mountain at Disney World. She learned to play Galaxians. She learned to use a computer. She took flying lessons.

Flying had been Ed Byars' hobby since he and Betsy met. For thirty-five years their vacations included visiting places where Ed could fly his sailplane. Betsy's job on these excursions was to run along beside the plane as it was towed for take-off and hold the wing level. Finally Betsy decided to get a pilot's license herself. She took her first flying lesson on April Fool's Day, 1983. In 1984 she got her license. "I am as proud of that as of anything in my writing career."

One day Betsy was sitting on the porch of the log cabin where she now does much of her writing. She looked up to see a large blacksnake wrapped around a beam. She named the snake Moon (because it was hanging above her head) and decided to write a book about being an author. She called it *The Moon and I.*

Here is how Betsy goes about writing a book. First she starts with a title page. In fact, she has a drawer full of title pages which she sometimes reads through for inspiration. When she begins a book, she spends a lot of time just sitting and staring while she works out the details of the plot. Then she begins writing, rapidly at first while she is full of enthusiasm, then more slowly. The next stage the book goes through is rewriting, when she polishes each sentence, trying to make the ideas which are so interesting and funny in her mind come out that way on paper.

The next step is to let her children read the manuscript and criticize it. They let her know where their interest lags by drawing a small arrow pointing downward in the margin. Betsy sometimes has dreams in which she gets a book review which is entirely blank except for the very center of the page, where there is a small arrow pointing downward.

Betsy likes the independence of being a writer. She sets her own hours and can decide her own topics to write about. It takes some self-discipline to get started, and she often stalls a lot before actually sitting down to work. Once she does start writing, she enjoys it, and has no problem sticking to her task.

By doing most of her writing in the winter, Betsy can be free to go on flying expeditions with her husband in the summer. This involves putting the sailplane together, taking it apart, taping and polishing it, and driving a thirty-five foot trailer around the country. Her other hobbies are reading, traveling, music, needlepoint, and crossword puzzles.

Betsy finds ideas for her books everywhere—from her own children, from newspaper headlines, from the hobbies she enjoys. Her books are realistic stories about young people and the problems they face. She is very sensitive and writes with a mixture of humor and deep feeling. She is especially good at creating unforgettable characters.

Betsy's books have been translated into nine different languages, and several of them have been made into television movies. She gets about two hundred letters from children each week.

Betsy has said that without her own children and the many story ideas they gave her, she might never have written children's books. When she first began her career, she wanted to write mystery books. It's an ambition she has finally fulfilled. In 1994 she did publish a mystery, but for children, not adults. *The Dark Stairs!* A Herculeah Jones Mystery, is the first of a series that is sure to be as popular as her Bingo Brown and Blossom Family books.

Notes:

Page 61   "I sewed fast..." Anne Commire, ed., *Something About the Author* (Gale Research Co., 1987), vol. 46, p. 36.

Page 63   "One of the best gifts..." Betsy Byars, *The Moon and I* (Julian Messner, 1991), p.

Page 64   "The important thing..." Commire, *Something About the Author*, p. 36.

                "The only thing..." Ibid., p. 37.

Page 67   "For me, reading books..." Byars, *The Moon and I,* p. 27.

Page 68   "I am as proud of that..." Commire, *Something About the Author,* p. 45.

For further reading about Betsy Byars:

Byars, Betsy. *The Moon and I.* Englewood Cliffs, NJ: Julian Messner, 1991.

Collier, Laurie and Joyce Nakamura, eds. *Major Authors and Illustrators for Children and Young Adults.*Detroit: Gale Research Co., 1993. p. 405-408.

Commire, Anne, ed. *Something About the Author.* vol. 46. Detroit: Gale Research Co., 1987

Cooper, Ilene. "The Booklist Interview: Betsy Byars." *Booklist,* January 15, 1993: 906-907.

Books for Young Readers by Betsy Byars:

1962 Clementine

1965 The Dancing Camel

1966 Rama the Gypsy Cat

1967 The Groober

1968 The Midnight Fox

1969 Trouble River

1970 The Summer of the Swans

1971 Go and Hush the Baby

1972 The House of Wings

1973 The Eighteenth Emergency

1973 The Winged Colt of Casa Mia

1974 After the Goat Man

1975 The Lace Snail

1976 The TV Kid

1977 The Pinballs

1978 The Cartoonist

1979 Goodbye, Chicken Little

1980 The Night Swimmers

1981 The Cybil War

1982 The Animal, the Vegetable, and John D. Jones

1982 The Two-Thousand-Pound Goldfish

1983 The Glory Girl

1984 The Computer Nut

1985 Cracker Jackson

1986 The Not-Just-Anybody Family

1986 The Blossoms Meet the Vulture Lady

1986 The Golly Sisters Go West

1987 The Blossoms and the Green Phantom

1987 A Blossom Promise

1988 Beans on the Roof

1988 The Burning Questions of Bingo Brown

1989 Bingo Brown and the Language of Love

1990 Bingo Brown, Gypsy Lover

1990 Hooray for the Golly Sisters!

1991 Seven Treasure Hunts

1991 Wanted...Mud Blossom

1992 Bingo Brown's Guide to Romance

1992 Coast to Coast

1993 McMummy

1994 The Dark Stairs: a Herculeah Jones Mystery

1994 The Golly Sisters Ride Again

JEAN LITTLE
A Different Perspective

"I am not cross-eyed. I have corneal opacities and eccentric pupils."

Ten-year-old Jean Little flung the words angrily at the bully who had teased her daily in the schoolyard. The retort so surprised him, he stopped his name-calling and, for once, did not chase her home.

Jean learned a lasting lesson. "I had found out what mere words could do. I would not forget."

Flora Jean Little was born in 1932 in Taiwan where her parents, both doctors, were medical missionaries. Mission work was a family tradition. Jean's maternal grandparents had gone to Taiwan in 1892. Her Aunt Gretta spent fifty-one years there.

Jean was the second of four children. She was born with scars on her corneas. Her eyes were so cloudy her pupils couldn't be seen. Although she responded to light by turning toward it, her parents believed her to be blind. It wasn't until she was four months old that Jean reached for an object, showing that she did have some sight.

In spite of her poor vision, Jean was an active child—climbing trees, playing with her two brothers and the other children of the neighborhood.

Most of all, Jean loved stories, and she was surrounded by relatives who were always ready to read to her. One of her first words was "book-a."

Jean couldn't wait until she was old enough for school to learn to read. She begged her mother to teach her. Her mother kept putting her off, telling her "soon." Jean wondered whether "soon" would ever become "now."

Then one day Mrs. Little led Jean into one of the house's unused rooms. Jean saw a chart with pictures cut from magazines labeled with large dark words—cat, dog, bird. She examined large print books sent from Canada. Best of all, she sat at a specially-made desk with a slanted top which let her bring her eyes close to her work. Now, at last, Mrs. Little could begin to teach Jean to read.

Jean's eye problems were severe. She had strabismus—her eyes could not focus together on one object. When she looked at something with her right eye, the left one would turn in toward her nose. She also had nystagmus—her eyes quivered. To Jean it looked as though the letters on the page were jiggling. Her scarred corneas made it necessary to hold the book very close to her eyes in order to see the print at all.

Refusing to be defeated, Jean learned to read. From then on she was seldom without a book in her hands.

When Jean was seven, the family moved to Hong Kong where her father had been appointed superintendent of a hospital. Jean's parents took her to consult a Chinese eye specialist. The specialist prescribed glasses—one pair for reading and another pair for distance. Jean couldn't tell the difference—but she loved having glasses. They were a grown-up thing.

With her new glasses and special uniforms—sleeveless cotton dresses in pastel colors with white rick-rack trim and matching underpants—Jean looked like all the other foreign children at Hong Kong's Peak school. When she held her book up to her nose to read, however, the other children laughed at her. "I was gradually learning that if you were different, nothing good about you mattered. And I had not really understood, until now, that I was different."

The family's stay in Hong Kong was brief. Mrs. Little and the children moved to Canada so Jean could attend special classes for visually-impaired children. Jean's father stayed behind to complete his year of mission service.

The Toronto Sight-Saving class Jean was enrolled in was just what she needed. Everything in the classroom was designed to help children who could not see well. The tilt-top desks were movable. There was fat yellow chalk for the green chalkboard. Learning was so easy for Jean in this class she skipped first grade and went right into second.

In the fall of 1940, Jean's father returned from his work in Hong Kong and, later, Japan. Home for good at last, he moved the family to Guelph, Ontario—the city where he had lived as a boy.

Jean's eye doctor recommended that she be sent to a school for the blind. However, the teacher of her Sight-Saving class thought Jean should not be taught to think of herself as blind. Instead, she should be placed in a regular classroom where she could learn to fit herself into the sighted world.

It was a big change for Jean. She skipped third grade. She went from a class of twelve to a class of forty-one. She no longer had a desk that could be moved to enable her to see the blackboard, and the teacher's writing on the board was invisible to her.

Jean's new teacher tried to be helpful, but the class was unfriendly. Jean was too different. She was cross-eyed. She read with her nose in her book. Because print was easier for her to read, she didn't have to do the cursive exercises everyone else labored over.

With no friends, left out of games, taunted in the schoolyard, chased home by bullies, Jean would have been thoroughly miserable except for two things—the love of her family, and the friends she found in books.

Books made Jean feel she was not alone at a time when she was not happy at school and was not happy with herself. She described herself as a coward, a crybaby, and "a terrible liar."

One of Jean's favorite books was *The Secret Garden,* by Frances Hodgson Burnett. "Mary Lennox...was just like me—selfish, bad-tempered, lazy, and entirely alive." Ever since she had started school Jean had known she was different because of her vision. Here was a heroine who was also different. Jean pictured Mary Lennox as looking like herself. Unloved and unlovable, Mary changes and grows from within, learning to reach out and make friends. "Ever since it had first been read to me when I was seven, it had remained the most magical book I knew."

Jean first thought of becoming a writer at the age of ten. Unable to find a good enough book to read one afternoon, she sat down with a notebook and a pencil and began to write an adventure story about a boy and his dog. Not allowing her family to disturb her, Jean wrote until she had filled the entire notebook.

As she wrote, Jean noticed that she had used the same adjective twice in a paragraph, and she changed it to another. "In that instant, I had started to turn into a writer."

When Jean was in sixth grade her teacher had the class keep journals. They were to record the events of their daily lives. Jean started out writing the real happenings of her life, but before long she became bored, and started to exaggerate.

Jean was horrified when the teacher collected the journals—hers was all lies. After reading them, the teacher told the class they were rubbish—too boring and stilted. The students didn't understand the criticism. They had been told to write about their lives, and their lives were boring.

The only journal the teacher had enjoyed was Jean's. "At least," she told the class, "hers was entertaining."

Jean was happy. Entertaining the teacher was far more important to her than being good at arithmetic.

Jean had a gift for looking at familiar stories in new ways. When Jean's eighth grade class discussed the Bible story of the Prodigal Son, she argued with the teacher about the importance of the older brother in the parable. Unable to make her idea clear, Jean spent all her free time during the day working on a poem explaining her thoughts. When she showed the poem to the teacher, he was impressed. Jean had made him see the story differently. Someday, he predicted, Jean would be a writer.

Jean was still very lonely. She had not yet learned how to reach out to make friends. Then she began attending meetings of a group called "Canadian Girls in Training" at her church. What they were in training for, Jean never learned. She did learn to love these meetings, however, for here she felt accepted for the first time. "Nobody had said 'cross-eyed' once. What was nicer was that I felt nobody had even thought it."

These meetings helped to give Jean much needed confidence. She became more outgoing, and when she entered high school the students seemed friendlier. The other girls helped make things easier for her. Jean finally began to feel accepted by her classmates.

Jean's father was happy that she was interested in writing. He thought poems were important, and he always took the time to read Jean's. He often suggested ways he thought they could be made better. Although Jean tried his suggestions, she was not always convinced he was right.

One criticism Mr. Little made was of Jean's choice of topics. She loved to write about pixies and sunsets. Her father thought this was foolish. "Write about what you know," he admonished her.

Angry, Jean went to her room and wrote a story about a girl and her father—and elves. Later she had to admit she enjoyed writing about the girl and her father more than the elves.

When Jean was fifteen, her father collected all the poems she had written since the age of twelve and went over them carefully with her, changing some lines, correcting meter, adding some words and phrases of his own.

When all the poems had been discussed and edited, Mr. Little found a local artist to illustrate them. Then he had the collection printed and bound.

Jean was delighted, even though she realized many of the poems were awkward. She disliked most of the changes her father had made, but she didn't tell him that. She was deeply grateful for his love of her work and his pride in her.

In 1949, when Jean was seventeen years old, her first published writing appeared in *Saturday Night*, Toronto's weekly magazine. She had written two Christmas poems, "Mary" and "Joseph." Her father was so impressed by them he sent them to the magazine. When they were published and her father read the printed poems to Jean "...his voice broke. I knew why I wanted to be a writer."

Jean struggled during her last years of high school. Her poor vision made it difficult to keep up with her work. It was necessary to work with tutors and to need an extra year to graduate. When she announced she wanted to continue her education at Victoria College in the University of Toronto, her father tried to talk her out of it. Although he knew how intelligent she was, he thought her poor sight would make her unable to handle the work.

Jean was insistent. What harm could there by in letting her try? Her father agreed to let her have a chance, and Jean enrolled in the University of Toronto for the fall semester of 1951.

Jean's father was very interested in her studies. He read and criticized her essays. He did his own research on the topics she was writing about, and he challenged her to think deeper and harder. When Jean received lower grades than she had hoped he encouraged her. He pointed out that she was there to improve, not to be praised.

Jean sometimes resented her father's nagging, but "before the year was over, I had the A Dad had bullied me into earning."

Jean spent the summer after her first year of college writing a book.

Let Me Be Gentle was the story of a family coming to terms with the youngest child's mental retardation. Jean was pleased with her efforts, and with high hopes she sent the manuscript to a publisher.

"I got a lovely rejection letter from Jack McClelland. He said my book was too short, too chopped up, and lacked focus. He also said I had talent and should keep writing."

Jean's father died while undergoing surgery during her second year of college. She felt the loss deeply, knowing how much his constant encouragement had helped her.

With determination and hard work, Jean finished college in four years. She graduated in 1955 and turned her thoughts toward earning a living. She attended summer training courses in Montreal and Utah to prepare to teach children with physical handicaps. She was hired by the Guelph Crippled Children's Centre to teach a small class. Jean liked the work and was a good teacher. But it troubled her that she could not find the kind of books she wanted to read to her students.

Jean knew there was a need for books about handicapped children who met challenges, made friends, and lived happy lives. She wanted children like her students to see themselves represented in fiction.

Jean's first published book, *Mine For Keeps,* was written for her handicapped students. The main character is much like Jean, and many of the incidents in the book are taken from her own experiences. She worked hard and long on the book, writing and rewriting until satisfied.

Uncertain about how to find a publisher, Jean asked a librarian friend who suggested she send the manuscript to the Little, Brown Canadian Children's Book Award contest. To Jean's great delight, her book won the $1,000 prize and was accepted for publication. The notification letter was signed by Jack McClelland—the same person who had rejected her first manuscript nine years before and encouraged her to keep writing.

Jean knew that she could not pursue her writing career and continue to teach at the same time. With some regret, but with her typical determination, she left teaching to pursue her dream of becoming an author.

When Jean was thirty years old she developed glaucoma in her left eye. She had three unsuccessful operations to relieve the pressure that caused her pain and further loss of vision. Finally, the eye had to be removed. Jean was fitted for a plastic eye that was held in place by her own muscles so its movement was coordinated with her right eye. After thirty years she was no longer cross-eyed.

Jean's life has been filled with friends, travel, and awards for her books. She has visited England. She lived in Japan for two years with a friend who taught in a mission school there. She and several other authors founded CANSCAIP—the Canadian Society of Children's Authors, Illustrators, and Performers—a national organization which now has hundreds of members. In 1976 she won the $5,000 Canada Council Children's Literature Prize for *Listen to the Singing*. With the prize money she purchased a car her mother drove for her. "The idea of my purchasing my first automobile just as I lost my sight had its darkly comic side," Jean said later, but it wasn't at all funny to her at the time. She had begun to develop glaucoma in her right eye, and knew that eventually she would totally lose her vision.

Fearing blindness, Jean became severely depressed. The reality of her situation struck her fully one summer night when a companion commented on the beauty of the stars. Jean had never been able to see the entire star-filled sky, but she had always been able to spot five or six of the very brightest stars. Now she couldn't make out a single one. The realization that she might never see them again hit her hard.

After several weeks of despair, Jean was listening one night to a recording of the novel *Watership Down*. Suddenly she realized that she could see the scene being described perfectly in her mind. Her lost stars were restored to her by this "talking book."

From then on things never seemed as bleak. Jean was able to adjust to her coming blindness and move on.

Finding a way to write was perhaps the most difficult. She was struggling with a book about a boy whose father dies of cancer. There were times when Jean thought it would never get written. Her Braille skills were not perfected. She couldn't see well enough to correct her mistakes on a typewriter. Eventually, she tried a dictaphone. It was awkward—she had to dictate every punctuation mark and specify each new paragraph. To go back and change a sentence, she had to make a whole new tape. Revising became a little easier when she learned to record from one tape machine to another, but the whole process was cumbersome.

But Jean's struggle to write this book was rewarded. *Mama's Going to Buy You a Mockingbird* was named Children's Book of the Year for 1985 by the Canadian Library Association.

Jean was ready to solve her next problem—finding a way to get around alone outside her own house. She wrote to The Seeing Eye in Morristown, New Jersey to apply for a guide dog. When she was accepted, she began a rigorous exercise program in preparation for handling her dog. Guide dogs are big and strong, and their owners must be in good physical shape to control them.

Jean spent three weeks in New Jersey learning to work with Zephyr, a golden retriever. When she returned home, she could go for walks, visit friends on her own, and travel. Zephyr not only guided her across streets, he helped locate curbs and stairs, find an empty chair when they entered a room, follow other people, and return to the right hotel room. With him, Jean felt in command of most situations.

Jean still needed a practical system for writing her books. The dictaphone method was too difficult and time-consuming. She heard a science program on the radio that mentioned a "talking word processor" which would soon be on the market. Jean wanted to know more about this new machine. She told all her friends and relatives to be alert for more information. A fellow writer soon sent Jean the information she needed. A talking computer had been developed by a blind inventor who lived in Hamilton, Ontario—a city not far from Guelph. SAM (the letters stand for Synthetic Audio Micro) had a voice synthesizer which read back the words that had been typed. Jean visited the inventor for a demonstration and knew this was the solution to her problem.

SAM was expensive. Jean received donations from family and friends, service clubs and women's groups in Guelph. A group of children raised money to purchase the necessary software.

SAM made the process of writing easier for Jean, but she had always known what to write in order to please her audience. Among the many awards her books have received, one of the most meaningful to Jean was the 1974 Vicky Metcalf Award, given by the Canadian Authors Association for a body of work inspirational to Canadian boys and girls. Jean counts some of the most outstanding current authors for children among her friends. To be honored by her fellow writers for her work is a great distinction.

In 1985, Jean received the Ruth Schwartz Award, a prize awarded by a jury of children. The children who read Jean's books are her most important critics, and their enjoyment of her work is her greatest reward.

As a child, Jean was often made to feel different because people saw her handicap instead of her personality. Through her books, Jean helps her readers see that the feelings, thoughts and actions of a handicapped person are not so different from their own.

Jean especially enjoyed a letter she once received in response to her first book, *Mine For Keeps*: "Dear Miss Little, You'd think Sally was me."

"That," said Jean Little, "was what I had been trying to tell her."

Notes:

Page 71   "I am not cross-eyed..." Jean Little, *Little by Little*
           (Toronto: Viking Kestrel, 1984), p. 113
           "I had found out what mere words..." Ibid.
Page 79   "I was gradually learning..." Ibid., p. 36
Page 80   "Mary Lennox was just like me..." Jean Little, "Home-
           coming," *The Horn Book Magazine* (May/June, 1991),
           p. 290.
           "Ever since it had been read to me..." Jean Little, *Stars
           Come Out Within* (Toronto: Viking, 1990), p. 259.
           "In that instant..." Little, *Little By Little*, p. 119.
Page 81   "At least..." Ibid., p. 123.
Page 82   "Nobody had said..." Ibid., p. 133.
Page 83   "...his voice broke..." Ibid., p. 177.
           "before the year was over..." Ibid., p. 202.
Page 84   "I got a lovely rejection..." Ibid., p. 206
Page 85   "The idea of my purchasing..." Little, *Stars Come Out
           Within*, p. 111.
Page 88   "Dear Miss Little..." Jean Little, "The People in Books",
           The Horn Book Magazine (April,1966), p. 162.
           "That was what..." Ibid.

For further reading about Jean Little:

De Montreville, D. and E. D. Crawford, eds. *Fourth Book of Junior Authors and Illustrators.* New York: H. W. Wilson Co., 1978.

Little, Jean. *Little By Little.* Toronto: Viking Kestrel, 1984.

___. *Stars Come Out Within.* Toronto: Viking, 1990.

Books for Young Readers by Jean Little

1962 Mine for Keeps

1965 Home from Far

1966 Spring Begins in March

1968 Take Wing

1969 One to Grow On

1970 Look through My Window

1971 Kate

1972 From Anna

1975 Stand in the Wind

1977 Listen for the Singing

1984 Mama's Going to Buy You a Mockingbird

1985 Lost and Found

1986 Different Dragons

1986 Hey World, Here I Am!

1991 Once upon a Golden Apple

1992 Jess Was the Brave One

1993 Revenge of the Small Small

KATHERINE PATERSON
Vehicles of Hope

Katherine ran. The teasing and laughter followed her as she stumbled to the top of the hill. She found a tree to rest against, away from the other children who made fun of her second-hand clothes and her British accent. "Jap," they called her. "Spy." They wouldn't listen when she tried to explain that she was an American like them; that she had been brought up in China, America's ally in the war, not in Japan, the enemy. So Katherine, a timid nine-year-old, ran to a place where she could be alone to weave her fantasies and escape into her books.

Katherine Womeldorf was born October 31, 1932, in Qing Jiang, China. Her parents were Presbyterian missionaries. Katherine was the third of five children. Unlike the other foreigners in China at the time, the Womeldorf's lived in a Chinese neighborhood, not in a compound with other families of their own nationality. Katherine's first language was Chinese, although she soon spoke English as well.

The Womeldorf children were raised on Bible stories, and knew the people of the Old Testament well. They were brought up on the strict principles of the founders of the Presbyterian church. Service to others was one of the most important of these principles. One of Katherine's earliest memories is of her father mounting a donkey to ride from village to village to deliver food and medicine in times of famine and disease.

Another early memory is of her mother reading to her. Katherine learned to love books, and, because she could not bear not being able to read, she studied her pre-school picture books until she understood the words. When she entered first grade, she was a self-taught reader.

In 1937, when Katherine was five years old, her family returned to the United States as refugees fleeing Japan's invasion of China. Katherine attended first grade in Richmond, Virginia. She was shy and found it hard to make friends. When Valentine's Day was celebrated, she came home without any valentines. Katherine's mother never forgot how sad it made her. Many years later, she asked Katherine why she didn't write about the time she didn't get any valentines. "But, Mother," Katherine said, "All my stories are about the time I didn't get any valentines.

In 1938, the Womeldorfs were able to return to China, this time to the British sector in Shanghai. Living in the British compound gave Katherine an English accent, and cost her much of her fluency in the Chinese language.

When Katherine was seven and in second grade in the American school in Shanghai, she published her first piece of writing in the school newspaper.

Pat! Pat! Pat!
There is the cat.
Where is the rat?
Pat, pat, pat.

She also enjoyed writing stories, and was influenced by the books she read. By the time she was eight, she had taken a liking to the "Elsie Dinsmore" books—a series of moralistic tales—and her stories began to imitate these. They were not very good. There was no hint that Katherine would one day be an award-winning author.

When World War II made the Womeldorfs refugees for a second time, they returned to the United States permanently. Katherine's father served as a minister in many different churches in Virginia, North Carolina, and West Virginia. During Katherine's childhood, the family moved more than fifteen times, and Katherine attended thirteen schools.

Katherine was not only shy, she also had a strange accent, and wore clothes from the missionary barrel. Sometimes she came to school wearing an article of clothing one of her classmates had donated to charity. She thought differently from the other children, a result of living with the Chinese, the British, and the Hebrew people of the Bible. Unable to overcome these differences and make friends with her classmates, she sought comfort in books. When she wasn't escaping to the neighboring hillside, Katherine found a refuge in the school library. Here she discovered the books of Kate Seredy, Robert Lawson, and Rachel Fields.

At home her mother read over and over the few books the family owned. Katherine's favorites were *The Wind in the Willows,* the *Just So Stories, The Secret Garden,* and the poems and stories of A. A.

Milne. *Jo Boy* was another favorite, and it made a life-long impression on her—forever after she was unable to kill spiders or sweep down their webs.

Katherine was frequently in trouble as a child. She was so naughty she felt she had to strike a bargain with God, atoning for all her misdeeds by reading the Bible.

When she was eleven, Katherine discovered Marjorie Kinnan Rawlings' *The Yearling,* and thought it was the best book she had ever read. That same year she became a library aide at the Calvin H. Wiley School in Winston-Salem, North Carolina. Her duties were to help the librarian by shelving books and reading to the younger classes. Later she was allowed to file in the card catalog and paste circulation card pockets in new books. By the time she left that school she was helping to mend damaged books. Katherine was very proud of this job. She grew to love the paper, the ink, the bindings. She learned to respect and cherish books.

In 1950, Katherine entered King College, a small Presbyterian school in Bristol, Tennessee. Here she was introduced to the classics of literature—Shakespeare, and the poets John Donne and Gerald Manley Hopkins. As she had in her "Elsie Dinsmore" days, she began to imitate these authors in her own writing. These were masters of the English language, and it gave her excellent writing practice. She also discovered *The Chronicles of Narnia,* by C. S. Lewis, and read them out loud to her fellow choir members as they traveled by bus to Atlanta for a concert.

After graduating from college Summa cum laude (with highest honors) in 1954, Katherine taught elementary school in Lovettsville, Virginia for a year. She then went to the Presbyterian School of

Christian Education in Richmond, Virginia for a master's degree. She was asked by one of her teachers there if she had ever considered becoming a writer. Katherine answered that she had not—she was planning to become a missionary like her parents.

In 1957, Katherine went to Japan, where she lived for four years, first as a student at the Naganuma School for the Japanese language in Kobe, and then as a Christian Education Assistant to a group of eleven pastors in the rural areas of Shikoku Island. Katherine had reservations about this assignment. As a child, she had known the Japanese people as enemies of her Chinese friends and of the United States. A Japanese woman pastor whom she met in graduate school persuaded her to give the people of Japan a chance. Katherine was glad she followed this woman's advice. She found that she loved the Japanese, who were friendly and helpful.

In 1961, Katherine returned to Virginia. It was a difficult transition. She couldn't sleep in her soft American bed. Every night she got up and lay on the floor to sleep. She felt that her own family didn't really know her. She had adopted Japanese ways of thinking and expressing herself. "Language is not simply the instrument by which we communicate thought. The language we speak will shape the thoughts and feelings themselves."

Katherine was awarded a fellowship to study at Union Theological Seminary in New York City. She earned her second master's degree in 1962. On July 14, 1962, she married John Barstow Paterson, a Presbyterian minister. The couple settled in New Jersey, and from 1963 to 1965, Katherine taught sacred studies and English at the Pennington School for Boys in Pennington, New Jersey.

In 1964, Katherine's life changed in several ways. She began her writing career with a job writing religious curriculum, John Barstow, Jr., was born, and Katherine and John adopted their first daughter, Elizabeth Polin, who had been born in Hong Kong in 1962. Two years later Katherine had a second son, David Lord. The family was completed in 1968 when Mary Katherine, an Apache Kiowan, was adopted at the age of five months.

Now Katherine had four children under the age of five. Her days were spent cooking, cleaning, mending, and settling squabbles. She needed something for herself "that wasn't either eaten up, dirtied, or torn apart by the end of the day." Because she enjoyed reading fiction so much, she turned to writing it.

There was no room available for Katherine to use for a study. Even if there had been a private space for her, she needed to keep an eye on the children. So Katherine wrote in the middle of the busy household, during whatever free time she could find. John was a great support as she learned how to write. He read her first mediocre efforts and encouraged her. As she began to improve, he nagged her to keep at it, and he became her first editor. When the family moved to Takoma Park, Maryland, John asked Katherine to write plays for the Presbyterian Church's annual Christmas service.

In 1968, Katherine took an adult education class in writing. Each week she brought to class another chapter of what would become her first published novel, *The Sign of the Chrysanthemum.* It was a book of historical fiction set it Japan, but it was also the story of her first adopted daughter. Lin had been abandoned by her mother in Hong Kong. She once asked Katherine why her mother had given her away. Katherine could only tell her that her mother had wanted her to have a better life than she could provide. The conversation made Katherine wonder what it must be like to have a parent somewhere that you did not know. This question is the central idea of *The Sign of the Chrysanthemum.*

While writing the book, Katherine did not ask herself if American children would want to read about historical Japan. It was a story she needed to write because of its importance to her emotionally. For over two years she sent it out to publishers. Finally, after many rejections, it was read by an editor who had just returned from a trip to Japan. The editor wasn't sure the book would be a commercial success, but she thought it was important for children to read about such an unfamiliar culture. She accepted the book, and worked hard with Katherine on the revisions. It was published in 1973, nine years after Katherine first began to write seriously. The book was moderately successful in hardcover, and has sold very well ever since the paperback version was published.

Katherine's next book, *Of Nightingales that Sing,* was also a historical novel with a Japanese setting. Because she found plots difficult to construct, Katherine liked to use the events of history to build her stories around. When it was finished, she asked her children what kind of story they thought she should try next. They requested a mystery. Katherine was doubtful—mysteries are very difficult to plot, and plotting was her weak point. Then one night she had a dream. She saw a boy on the second floor of a dark storehouse. As he searched for something, he heard a step on the stairs. He looked up to see a Japanese warrior puppet appear brandishing a sword. Behind him was the hooded figure of the puppeteer. Katherine woke up wondering what the boy had been looking for, and why the puppeteer seemed so menacing. She wrote *The Master Puppeteer* to find out what happened to the boy in her dream. Although she had been hesitant about trying to write a mystery, the book was named a runner-up for the Edgar Allan Poe Award given by the Mystery Writers of America. It also received the National Book Award.

During the time she was finishing these books, Katherine discovered she had cancer. She was operated on successfully, and was given a good prognosis for recovery. Soon afterwards, her son David's closest friend was struck by lightning and killed. Both events brought the reality of death home to Katherine, and she had a hard time coping with her emotions. She took the advice of a friend, and tried to work out her feelings by writing about them. When she reached the point where the character in her story had to die, Katherine couldn't write it. She discussed her reluctance with her friend, who suggested that perhaps it was the idea of her own death Katherine couldn't face, not the fictional character's. Katherine returned to the book with renewed determination to write the scene. By the end of the day the chapter was done, and within a few weeks the whole book was finished. *Bridge to Terebithia* was published in 1977, and won the Newbery Award, given by the American Library Association for the year's most distinguished contribution to children's literature.

In 1975, while Katherine was writing *Bridge to Terebithia*, the Paterson children were watching a television report one evening on the plight of homeless children in Cambodia. They wanted to help, and asked their parents to adopt one of these refugees. Katherine and John felt they couldn't adopt another child, but they did decide to take in two Cambodian boys as foster children for a temporary period. The boys' stay stretched from the original two weeks to over two months. They soon stopped being on their best behavior and problems began to arise. Katherine found herself avoiding dealing with the children's problems; she knew they would soon leave her care. Her realization that she was treating them differently from her own children led her to think about the thousands of foster children in the United States who are treated by our society as "disposable." She decided to write a book about a foster child, *The Great Gilly Hopkins,* which won the 1978 Newbery Honor Award, was set in Takoma Park, where Katherine had lived for thirteen years—the longest she had ever lived in one place.

In 1979, the Patersons moved to Norfolk, Virginia, where John served as pastor of Lafayette Presbyterian Church until 1986. Virginia had been the setting for *Bridge to Terebithia.* It was also where Katherine had first taught after graduating from college. Perhaps it was this return to a familiar location which awoke memories of her own childhood. Katherine's next book, *Jacob Have I Loved,* was a story of sibling jealousy, and contained many of the feelings Katherine had as the middle child of five. Katherine received her second Newbery Award for this book, which was published in 1981.

In the early 1980's, Katherine took a trip to China. She wanted to visit the places she had known as a child to absorb the atmosphere of this land which was to be the setting of her next novel. With *Rebels of the Heavenly Kingdom,* Katherine returned to historical fiction, which she loved. China was also the setting for *The Tale of the Mandarin Ducks.* Other historical novels were *Lyddie,* set in the cotton mills of New England, and *Park's Quest,* which was inspired by Katherine's participation in the National Women's Conference to Prevent Nuclear War, and by the experience of family friends who lost a son in the Vietnam War.

In 1988, the Patersons moved to Vermont, where Katherine continues to publish at least one book every year. She also enjoys several hobbies, including reading, swimming, tennis, and sailing.

Katherine's writing has been influenced by her experiences in China and Japan, by her adolescence in the American South, and by her strong biblical heritage. The characters in her books begin as aspects of Katherine herself. She is protective of her books while writing them, and will not discuss them with family or friends until they are finished. Her first reader is always John.

Katherine remembers what it was like to be a child. She recalls being a "weird little kid," and an outsider, who entertained herself by reading and writing, and by fantasizing a lot. "...There are few things, apparently, more helpful to a writer than having once been a weird little kid."

Katherine writes for children because she loves their enthusiasm. Children use their imaginations eagerly as they enter into the book's world. They will read a book they love over and over, and approach new books with great expectations. Katherine finds that she is able to write well for children, and it is a joy for her to do so. She considers life and death matters to be appropriate topics for children's books, believing that children need to know the truth about life, so they can decide how they will live. She writes about the difficulties of life, but she does so with optimism.

Katherine writes about issues that touch her deeply, and her goal is to write a story that will satisfy the type of reader she was as a child. She remembers how she longed for a book that made her feel understood. "I keep learning that if I am willing to go deep into my own heart, I am able, miraculously, to touch other people at the core."

Katherine has always been an avid reader of fiction. Both children and adults read fiction for the same reason, she believes. They want to experience the unfamiliar, to expand their knowledge and feelings, to explore different ways of looking at the world. "...books, fiction, give us practice in life that we've never had to live through before, so when the time comes, we have in a sense been through that experience before....Books are great vehicles of hope for us and help and instruct us in all the good ways."

Some readers and reviewers have complained that her books often do not have happy endings. Katherine takes such comments seriously, and understands that children have a strong desire for the conventional "happily ever after conclusion." In her realistic stories, however, such endings are seldom possible. Instead, she writes what she believes are hopeful endings, in which her main characters receive reassurance, and their pain is not trivialized by easy solutions. Hope, to Katherine, is more than wishful thinking, it is a yearning for justice and truth.

Notes:

Page 94   "But, Mother..." Anne Commire, ed., *Something About the Author* (Gale Research Co., 1988), vol. 53, p. 121.

Page 97   "Language is not..." Ibid., p. 124.

Page 98   "that wasn't either..." Linda T. Jones, "Profile: Katherine Paterson" *Language Arts* (February, 1981), p. 191.

Page 102   "...there are few things..." *Something About the Author,* p. 121.

"I keep learning..." Katherine Paterson, "What Writing Has Taught Me" *The Writer* (August, 1990), pp. 9-10.

Page 103   "...books, fiction, give us practice..." Bryan Ryan, ed., *Major Twentieth Century Authors: a Selection of Sketches from Contemporary Authors* (Gale Research, 1991), p. 2299.

For further reading about Katherine Paterson:

Gallo, Donald R., ed. *Speaking for Ourselves.* Urbana, IL: National Council of Teachers of English, 1990.

Paterson, Katherine. *Gates of Excellence: On Reading and Writing Books for Children.* New York: Elsevier-Dutton Publishing Co., Inc., 1981.

___. *The Spying Heart: More Thoughts on Reading and Writing Books for Children.* New York: Dutton Children's Books, 1990

Books for Young Readers
by Katherine Paterson

1973 Sign of the Chrysanthemum

1974 Of Nightingales that Sing

1976 The Master Puppeteer

1977 Bridge to Terebithia

1978 The Great Gilly Hopkins

1979 Angels and Other Strangers: Family Christmas Stories

1981 Jacob Have I Loved

1983 Rebels of the Heavenly Kingdom

1985 Come Sing, Jimmy Jo

1988 Park's Quest

1990 The Tale of the Mandarin Ducks

1991 Lyddie

1992 The King's Equal

1994 Flip-Flop Girl

RICHARD PECK
Educating, Entertaining, Encouraging

Richard Peck's childhood was filled with stories. When the family gathered, his grandparents and aunts and uncles told stories of their growing-up years. At his father's gas station the old-timers passed the day swapping tales, and Richard was their eager audience. At home, his mother's voice brought to life the stories in books. And then there was the radio. Like other boys his age, Richard listened avidly to the adventures of "Jack Armstrong, All American Boy," "The Green Hornet," "Inner Sanctum." Words fascinated Richard— they created characters and opened doors into new worlds.

Richard Peck was born April 5, 1934, in Decatur, Illinois. He and his younger sister, Cheryl, grew up amid a large extended family. There they learned American middle-class values: take responsibility for your own acts, respect the wisdom of your elders, recognize your duty to others.

Richard was born during the Great Depression. His father and uncle had lost their automobile dealership in the economic crisis. His father then managed a Phillips 66 gas station. He supplemented the family's income by raising calves and chickens on farms owned by relatives and by doing lots of fishing. Richard's mother baked and canned. She cured meat in the garage and prepared sausage on the porch.

By the time Richard was seven the United States had entered World War II. Richard's first grade class was involved in the war, too. Richard followed the battles with pins on wall maps. He helped with recycling campaigns. He bought Defense Stamps every week. During recess he played dive bomber. He also helped the Cub Scouts collect newspapers for the war effort, but they complained about his slowness. He kept sitting down on the curbs to read the papers.

When the war was discussed at home, Richard's father recalled his service in the first World War. Richard listened to his father argue that the government was manipulating public opinion—that the United States should not be involved in the war. It was a lesson for Richard—not all adults thought alike.

When Richard was in fifth grade, the war ended. Global news suddenly became less important and school work became the focus of Richard's attention. By the time he entered junior high school, Richard took school seriously. He always came to school with his homework completed, not because he was especially good, but because he was afraid not to. Richard worked hard to get the highest grades possible so that he could earn a scholarship to college.

Richard had a paper route to teach him responsibility. He was sent to dance class with other neighborhood children so that he could learn how to behave on social occasions. He and his friends went to dance class without complaint because it seemed like a grown-up thing to do. "I touched all these bases because from early times I really thought you had a lot of dues to pay before they'd let you into adulthood. For middle-class kids it was very much that kind of era, but I think I believed it more than most."

Latin was an elective subject in Richard's school, but when the Latin teacher confronted Richard in the hallway and let him know she expected him to sign up for the class, he did. It wasn't an easy subject, but it was a rewarding one. Richard credits his Latin class with unlocking the secrets of the English language and giving him the confidence to be a writer.

Richard had many other memorable teachers in junior high. His history teacher taught him to outline by requiring that he outline the textbook. He can still recite the battles of the Revolutionary War in sequence. His industrial arts teacher had the class go home and rewire electrical appliances. They were to bring in the frayed wires and broken plugs as proof the assignment was completed. Richard was impressed by this teaching technique which countered the young teenager's yearning for independence with a task that drew him back to his home and family.

Richard played the sousaphone in the junior high marching band. When the music teacher assigned him the instrument because he was the only student tall enough for it, Richard agreed. He could see that if he played the sousaphone he wouldn't have to practice—it was too big to carry home each day. The music teacher outguessed him, however. He delivered the sousaphone to Richard's house every Friday for a weekend of practice. Every Monday Richard's father delivered him and the sousaphone to school.

Richard remembered these teachers all his life. They were demanding; the ones from whom he learned the most. He had other teachers, of course, but they expected less from him, and were soon forgotten.

In high school, Richard was still striving for all A's so he could earn that college scholarship. He worked at the local A & P on Saturdays, bagging groceries for $7.45 a day. For recreation, there were dances and movies. Richard and his friends went to the movies as often as they could. Many of the characters in the films he saw as a teenager later became models for characters in his books.

Richard did not seriously consider a career as a writer when he was in high school. "I'd probably already heard that writers can't make a living at it, and making a living was a high priority in Decatur."

Still, writing was a secret ambition, and Richard looked at his high school subjects in terms of their potential contribution to a career as an author. The study of history provided something to say. Latin class taught him how to say it. Geography gave him settings for his stories.

A trip to New York City when he was sixteen also gave Richard a glimpse of what his future might hold. As he explored New York, he felt that this was the place he was meant for to live. He decided that one day he would make this city his home.

Senior year English was Richard's most influential high school class. It was taught by the most exacting teacher he had had yet. She insisted that students research and document the subjects they wrote on. She taught that the mastery of grammar was essential to a writer. In this class, Richard learned to edit and rewrite his work and to honor deadlines. It was an invaluable course in the craft of writing.

In his English literature courses Richard was exposed to many different authors and poets. It struck him as odd, though, that all of them were dead. Contemporary authors were not taught, making Richard wonder whether writing could be a modern occupation at all. Maybe an author's writing was not taken seriously until he or she had died.

The state of Illinois did have a famous contemporary writer to its credit, however. During high school Richard encountered the poetry of Vachel Lindsay—a famous modern writer. Olive Lindsay Wakefield, the poet's sister, gave a reading of her brother's poems in Decatur. Richard was so impressed, he wrote her a letter asking permission to call on her in her home in Springfield. It was a memorable visit. Mrs. Wakefield lived in the Lindsay family home— the house Vachel had lived and worked in. Mrs. Wakefield was a gracious but lonely woman. Her concern for history, her wisdom, and her eccentricity remained with Richard and formed the basis of many characters in his novels.

In the spring of his senior year, Richard learned that he had achieved his long-held goal. He won a scholarship to DePauw University in Indiana. In Decatur, the people who shared Richard's interests were the teachers. Because he admired so many of them, he decided to pursue a teaching career.

For an English major, nothing could be more fun than the opportunity to travel to England to study for a year. Richard spent his junior year of college at Exeter University in Devon, England, studying literature and British history. It was 1954, and he was twenty years old. Everything was exciting—the trip over on an ocean liner, the picturesque towns, the good friends he acquired, the fulfillment of his dream of going to distant places. And once again, Richard absorbed potential characters and settings that would one day become part of his novels.

Richard returned to DePauw and finished his senior year in the spring of 1956. After graduation, he found that he could not get a teaching job. No school would hire him while he was subject to the draft, so he looked for other types of employment. His first job, in Gary, Indiana, was as an "executive trainee" for the phone company. Part of his duties included removing pay phones from off-track betting offices, businesses run by organized crime, and other illegal establishments.

Within a year, Richard was drafted into the Army and assigned to a missile base in Germany. Richard didn't want to spend his time going on field maneuvers or standing guard duty. With some bluffing and finagling of records, he managed to get himself installed as a clerk in the base office. By the time the records were straightened out, Richard was already doing the job, and was allowed to stay in it.

After hearing the base chaplain give a poor sermon, Richard saw an opportunity to improve his situation further. He wrote a sermon and slipped it under the chaplain's door. He was delighted to hear his sermon delivered the following Sunday. Soon he was made the chaplain's assistant—a job which he expanded to include marriage counseling, writing sermons for chaplains of all denominations, and hearing soldiers' confessions. The problems the soldiers shared with him would later often turn up in his books.

When his two years of army service were up, Richard enrolled in Southern Illinois University to work toward a Master's degree. He had an assistantship which required him to teach a freshman writing course in the evening. Expecting a class of eighteen-year-olds, Richard was surprised, and a little flustered, to walk into a room full of adults, most of whom were older than he was. However, he enjoyed the class. The students were serious about their education—working hard, completing assignments on time, and participating actively in class discussions.

After additional graduate study at Washington University in St. Louis, Richard got his first job as a high school English teacher in 1961. Glenbrook, Illinois was an affluent suburb of Chicago. Richard discovered that his students were overindulged, self-centered, and unchallenged. They seemed to believe they would always get what they wanted, would always be safe in their suburban neighborhoods—isolated from the "real world" of the city.

Richard taught at Glenbrook for two years. Then, in 1963, he had an opportunity to work for Scott, Foresman, and Company in Chicago as a textbook editor. Here he learned why his high school textbooks contained so few modern writers. The publisher couldn't earn a profit if too much had to be paid for permission to reprint copyrighted work. If an author had died long ago, the copyright was expired and the work could be used without payment.

While working at Scott, Foresman, Richard and a friend wrote a guide to Chicago night life called *Old Town, A Complete Guide: Strolling, Shopping, Supping, Sipping.* Self-published, it was Richard's first printed work.

In 1965, Richard learned about an opening for an English teacher at a private school for academically gifted girls affiliated with Hunter College in New York City. Richard had wanted to live in New York for years. He applied for the job and was hired.

Richard loved teaching, and was inventive and inspired. He once stood on a desk to recite Marc Antony's emotional funeral oration from Shakespeare's *Julius Caesar.* When the school board decided that Harper Lee's *To Kill a Mockingbird* should be removed from the school library because it celebrated "white bourgeois values," Richard was appalled. He wrote the title and author on his classroom blackboard and told his students it was being banned for their own good. The students found copies and read the book, as he had known they would.

Teaching at Hunter College High School was even more difficult than it had been at Glenbrook. The students were uninterested in formal teaching. In fact, they were often absent from class in order to participate in political demonstrations. Deeply concerned about his students' welfare, Richard worried that they were too privileged, and were therefore failing to learn responsibility. He was also very troubled by his students' strong allegiance to their peer group. To be adult, he knew, meant being willing to think for yourself. He wondered how teenagers who refused to think or act differently from their peers would ever begin to grow up.

While teaching at Hunter, Richard recognized the need for a way to introduce modern authors to his students. This led to his first serious venture into publishing. With Ned E. Hoopes, another faculty member, he edited an anthology of contemporary fiction. *Edge of Awareness* was published in a paperback edition in 1966 by Dell Publishing Company. It is still in print, although it is used more now often in college classes than in high schools.

Richard had more work published in 1967. This time it was a series of writing activities for a Language Arts textbook. He was trying his hand at poetry, too. "Nancy", a poem about the interaction between a teacher and a student, was published in the *Saturday Review* in 1969. At the same time he was working on an anthology of poems, *Sounds and Silences: Poetry for Now.*

In 1969, Richard received a grant to serve as the assistant director of the Council for Basic Education. He took a year off from his teaching job and moved to Washington, D. C. The Council was a private organization dedicated to educational innovation. Richard's job was to write articles for the Council's newsletter and other publications. This provided a chance to hone his writing skills. He worked closely with the publications editor, who advised him as he rewrote and polished his articles. The success and satisfaction he experienced in this position convinced him he wanted to be a writer. He returned to teaching for one more semester. In 1971, he resigned from teaching, intending to become a novelist.

Most novelists keep their jobs until their books become established and produce income. Richard quit his job and *then* began to write his first novel. In four months it was finished. He carefully piled the pages in a shoebox and delivered it to the editor he had worked with on *Edge of Awareness. Don't Look and It Won't Hurt* was published in 1972.

When he is working on a novel, Richard does not follow any set schedule for writing. He finds that he gets more done in the late afternoon. He also finds that as he gets further into a novel, he gets more and more absorbed in the world he is creating. When he first started writing he thought he would spend all his time at home working. He didn't realize that it would be part of his job to go out and tell readers about his books.

About one quarter of Richard's time is spent traveling to schools and libraries to talk with teens, parents, and teachers about his novels. Sometimes he will write to a school before he visits and request that the students write a paper for him. He suggests that they write about an event in their lives that might fit into a novel. This lets him learn something about the students before he meets them. It also gives him a good idea of what issues are on teenagers' minds.

Many of the ideas in Richard's novels come from these papers and from the discussions he has with students during his visits. Richard collects names for his characters from readers' letters, school telephone books, and high school yearbooks. He "researches" dialogue by eavesdropping on conversations to keep up with teenagers' vocabulary. When he first started writing, he sometimes wondered where the idea for the next book would come from. Now he finds he gathers more ideas than he can use from the comments and questions of his readers.

The settings in Richard's books are all real—even the houses are buildings he has seen or been in. He never writes about a place he hasn't visited. This, he says, gives him a good excuse to travel, something he loves to do. He spends part of each year on a cruise ship, teaching creative writing, and giving lectures about the ports the ship visits. He not only collects scenes and characters from these cruises, he also gets to talk with the grandparents of his teenaged readers.

Richard has won many awards for his books. His novels have appeared on American Library Association lists of "notable books," "best books," and "best of the best books." He has received the Edgar Allan Poe Mystery Award twice, both times for books he did not consider mysteries. Several honors have been awarded him by state and national associations of English and writing teachers. In 1990, he received the prestigious Author Achievement Award given by the School Library Journal Young Adult Services Division. His long list of awards shows that not only teenagers love his books. Parents, teachers, and other authors also recognize the value and impact of his writing.

Several of Richard's books have been made into TV movies and full-length films. His first novel, *Don't Look and It Won't Hurt*, became the highly praised movie, *Gas, Food, Lodging*. *The Ghost Belonged to Me* became the Disney TV movie, *Child of Glass*. *Father Figure* and *Are You In the House Alone?* were also filmed. In each case, there were many changes in the story. Settings, characters, points of view, events, even endings were altered from Richard's original ideas. Richard did not like the changes; he felt the whole point of the original novel was often lost. However, when film makers buy the movie rights for a book, they also buy the right to make whatever changes they wish.

Richard Peck left teaching and became a writer because he couldn't teach the way he had been taught. The students, the curriculum, and the attitude of society had changed too much. He is grateful to his former students. What he learned from them about their needs, fears, hopes, and lifestyles, gave him the material he needed to develop stories that touched their lives. Peck believes adults have let young people down, allowing educational standards to become lax, and home life to become too permissive. In his books he tries to provide three important elements which he feels are lacking in many teenagers' lives—entertainment, ideas, and reassurance.

Notes:

Page 111   "I touched all these bases..." Donald R. Gallo, *Presenting Richard Peck* (Dell Publishing, 1993), p. 10.

Page 112   "I'd probably already heard..." Richard Peck, *Anonymously Yours* (Julian Messner, 1991), p. 57.

For further reading about Richard Peck:

Collier, Laurie and Joyce Nakamura, eds. *Major Authors and Illustrators for Children and Young Adults*. Detroit: Gale Research, 1993, pp. 1843-1847.

Commire, Anne, ed. *Something About the Author*. Detroit: Gale Research, 1989, vol. 55, pp. 126-138.

Gallo, Donald R. *Presenting Richard Peck*. New York: Dell Publishing, 1993.

Peck, Richard. *Anonymously Yours*. Englewood Cliffs, NJ: Julian Messner, 1991.

Sutton, R. A. "A Conversation With Richard Peck." School Library Journal, June, 1990, vol. 36, pp. 36-40.

Books for Young Readers by Richard Peck

1972 Don't Look and It Won't Hurt

1973 Dreamland Lake

1973 Through a Brief Darkness

1974 Representing Super Doll

1975 The Ghost Belonged to Me

1975 Ghosts I Have Been

1976 Are You In the House Alone?

1978 Father Figure

1979 Secrets of the Shopping Mall

1981 Close Enough to Touch

1983 The Dreadful Future of Blossom Culp

1985 Remembering the Good Times

1986 Blossom Culp and the Sleep of Death

1987 Princess Ashley

1988 Those Summer Girls I Never Met

1989 Voices After Midnight

1991 Unfinished Portrait of Jessica

1993 Bel-Air Bambi and the Mall Rats

1994 The Last Safe Place on Earth

Virginia Hamilton
Teller of Tales

Virginia grabbed hold of her grandfather's clenched fist as he lifted her off her feet. Laughing, she swung from the hand that had been permanently scarred shut in a fire at the gunpowder mill where he worked.

"Ever after, the raised Black fist became for me both myth and history, and they were mine...Grandpaw Perry was power—the fugitive, the self-made, the closed fist in which I knew was kept magic...."

Virginia Hamilton was born March 12, 1936, the youngest of five children. The family lived on a small farm in Yellow Springs, Ohio. Yellow Springs had once been a station on the Underground Railroad, and many of the town's residents, including Virginia's mother, were descended from runaway slaves.

Virginia's grandfather, her mother's father, had escaped from the state of Virginia at the age of five in 1857. The family had settled on farm land in Yellow Springs. When Virginia's parents married, they bought land from her mother's family. Virginia grew up next to her aunts, uncles, and cousins.

The family had a strong story-telling tradition. Whenever the relatives gathered the chief entertainment was the retelling of family history, often with considerable elaboration. If the storytellers forgot details of the events they were relating they made up their own. It was a process of creative remembering—merging fact and fiction—which Virginia came to call "rememory." "They thus created and recreated who they were and where they had come from and what they hoped to be."

These stories not only taught Virginia her family's history and traditions, they taught her about the values of society and of her family. She learned to think of her life and of her relationships to other people in terms of stories. Her grandfather told and retold the story of his escape from slavery so that his grandchildren would learn to cherish their freedom. Her mother told scary stories during storms to distract Virginia from her fear of thunder and to calm her down. Her mother also recounted terrible floods, so that the ordinary floods they sometimes experienced came to seem less frightening. Her aunts and uncles regaled her with the escapades of other family members, exaggerating freely, and never telling a story the same way twice.

Virginia's family had lived in Yellow Springs for generations, and were well-known to everyone in the community. Virginia could be on her own all day, roaming the countryside around her home. She could go to the local grocery store and treat her friends to snacks, charging them to her father's account.

Virginia, her brothers, sisters, and cousins, were sometimes enemies, sometimes friends. They practiced stilting on homemade stilts—an African tradition. They made their own Halloween costumes. They scared each other with tales of the "haunted" house they walked past on the way to and from school each day—a house that belonged to a family named Dies.

On their small hog farm, the Hamiltons raised enough food for their own use and sold the extra at the local market. Virginia helped her father on the farm. He dug long rows with the hoe and she would drop seeds in, spacing them carefully. Then her father with his hoe, and Virginia with her hands, would cover the seeds with dirt. Virginia and her father had a special relationship. As the youngest child, she was his favorite, and he spoiled her.

Virginia's father was in his fifties when she was born. He was a business school graduate who had worked as a janitor, railroad porter, and a gambling hall operator. By the time Virginia was born he was employed as the food service manager for Antioch College in Yellow Springs, a position which gave him faculty status at the school.

Virginia's father had a large collection of books, and she was encouraged to read. Books by Edgar Allan Poe, Franz Kafka, and Arthur Conan Doyle were some of her childhood reading. At school, Virginia won prizes for the number of books she read.

"Ever after [childhood], I have been an ardent reader, not only of books, but of most anything—old match covers, catalogs, whatever falls into my hands"

By the time she was nine or ten, Virginia was writing. It was a natural evolution, taken for granted by her teachers and family. Praised and encouraged by her teachers, Virginia knew by high school she wanted to be a writer.

Virginia was a good student. But in school she encountered a subtle form of racism. There were no Black teachers. The history of African Americans was taught only in terms of slavery events. Songs like "Old Black Joe" and "My Old Kentucky Home" reminded Virginia and her friends of their "place." It made the Black students feel they needed to do better than their white classmates. Virginia was motivated to do her best and became a leader in school.

In high school, Virginia wrote a play which her classmates performed for a senior assembly. She was clearly on her way to her goal of becoming a famous writer some day.

In 1952, Virginia was awarded a full scholarship to Antioch College in Yellow Springs, where she took writing and literature courses.

Virginia did well in her college courses. She enrolled in a co-op program, which enabled her to meet expenses by holding jobs between semesters. In between studying and working, she found time to write short stories. She also kept a card file of story ideas for future use. Influenced by magazines on Africa which she had seen at home, Virginia filled her card file with information about that continent. She made notes of different countries, climates, governments, population, tribal customs, languages. This became a way of exploring her connections to her ancestors.

Virginia participated in a psychology experiment while she was at college. The results of the experiment showed her to be "normal." She was disappointed, thinking it meant she was only "average." It caused her to spend a lot of time thinking about what being normal implied. Her conclusion was that "normal" meant something solid.

It was a foundation upon which to build.

Virginia received her Bachelor of Arts degree in 1955. After college, Virginia headed for New York City where she held a series of short-term jobs. She sang in nightclubs in Brooklyn and Manhattan. She played guitar for a dance band. She worked as a part-time bookkeeper. All during this time she continued to write.

Virginia never planned to write for children. She was trying to sell stories for adults. A friend remembered a short story Virginia had written in college—one that drew on some of the many facts she had learned about Africa. Perhaps that could be revised and made into a novel? Virginia began work on the book that would eventually be published as *Zeely,* her first novel.

At first, Virginia's life in New York City was lonely. When she wasn't working, she spent her time alone in her apartment writing. She made no friends and sometimes went days without talking to anyone. Her greatest pleasure was sitting by the banks of the Hudson River, letting the flow of the water renew her energy and sense of purpose.

In 1957, Virginia returned to Ohio to attend Ohio State University for two years. Afterwards, when back in New York City, she enrolled in the New School for Social Research, where she took a writing course. Here she met Arnold Adoff, who was studying poetry. Arnold and Virginia found they had a common interest in music—both enjoyed jazz. Soon they were dating, and in 1960 they married.

Virginia and Arnold agreed on a five-year plan. Arnold would teach and Virginia would devote five years to becoming a published author. If she failed, Arnold would take the next five years to try to succeed with his writing. Their plan worked differently than expected. In the first five years both became professional writers. Virginia was especially glad. She had worked as a bookkeeper and as a cost accountant, and she hated it. Now she would not have to go back to that drudgery.

While Virginia was working on *Zeely,* she and Arnold spent six months in Spain. The experience had a great influence on her book. She also had her first child during this time. Leigh was born in 1963. In 1967, the year *Zeely* was published, her second child, Jaime, was born.

In *Zeely,* all the characters use storytelling as a means of understanding themselves, their culture, and their society. Geeder, the main character, makes up stories about herself and her brother, and invents fantasies about their neighbor. This is her way of trying to control her life and explain her feelings. Zeely, the unusually tall neighbor who captures Geeder's imagination, tells stories to recreate her own life. Like Virginia, the book's characters interpret their lives through stories.

When *Zeely* was done, Virginia began a second book, *The House of Dies Drear.* Again, she drew on her own experiences. Yellow Springs had many houses which had been served as places for fugitive slaves in the days of the Underground Railroad. Virginia especially remembered the Dies house, which had seemed such a frightening place when she was a child. Combining this well-remembered setting with all she had learned from her father's collection of Conan Doyle books about the construction of mystery plots, Virginia produced a story of ghosts, murders, sliding panels, and secret tunnels. Published in 1968, *The House of Dies Drear* won the Edgar Allan Poe Award for best juvenile mystery.

Virginia next began what would eventually become *M. C. Higgins, the Great.* She wrote one chapter, then found that the story was not yet fully formed in her mind. She had a glimpse of a character, and a few incidents, but the whole story had not yet emerged. She put it aside and went on to other books.

Her next book, *The Time-Ago Tales of Jahdu,* was a collection of original stories told in folk-tale style. Again she was influenced by her family's love of stories, gossip, and tall tales.

Virginia grew dissatisfied with life in New York. The city was too stimulating. She had no time to think and no control over her life. She and Arnold decided to move back to Yellow Springs. In 1969 they returned to Ohio, bought two acres of the Hamilton family land, and built a house. The design for the house was taken from a magazine. It was made of redwood and glass. It had no windows— just sliding glass doors and clerestory lights. Here both Virginia and Arnold could work, and Virginia could be close to her birth family and re-connect to the rich family history.

Virginia's next book began with an idea that came to her when she saw a boy in a park playing hooky on a school day. Giving the boy the name Buddy Clark, Virginia started to write his story. Gradually, however, another character began to grow in her mind, and she found she had to rewrite the story to include him. He became the title character of the book, *The Planet of Junior Brown.*

Another collection of Jahdu stories, *Time-Ago Lost: More Tales of Jahdu*, followed. By the time this book was published in 1973, Virginia was ready to resume work on *M. C. Higgins, the Great*, the manuscript she had set aside five years earlier.

M. C. Higgins, the Great was published in 1974. The delay had been worthwile. This book earned Virginia more awards than most children's authors have ever won for a single book, including the Boston Globe-Horn Book Award, New York Times Outstanding Book of the Year, National Book Award, and the Newbery Medal.

Virginia's title characters, Zeely, Junior Brown, and M. C. Higgins, all have in common an exaggerated trait or behavior. Zeely is extraordinarily tall. Junior Brown is extremely fat. M. C. Higgins spends his days sitting on top of a flagpole. They are all surreal— bigger than life—rather than realistic. By employing such eccentricities, Virginia encourages her readers to explore the symbolism of the words, feelings and actions of each character.

The eight novels which followed *M. C. Higgins, the Great* all had African American female protagonists, five with psychic powers that could be used for the good of themselves, others, or the world. These unconventional characters are typical of Virginia's imagination.

The hardest part of writing for Virginia is just getting herself started. Sometimes she gets herself going by reading something by William Faulkner "...just to remind myself that it's hard work to create the simplicity that begins a story."

Sometimes she goes for a run on the high school track, imagining winning a race before stands of cheering people.

Once she does get started, Virginia writes in four to six hour stretches. "That's steady thinking and writing—work that causes wear and tear on the mind."

In addition to her novels and short story collections, Virginia has written several biographies and folklore anthologies. In each case, her intent has been to record the accomplishments of Black people, their struggle against oppression, and their cultural contributions.

Virginia writes for young children and teenagers as well as middle grade readers. Her first goal is to create an entertaining story. Her own beliefs enter her stories, because all her characters, real or imaginary, live within a social order. Her themes are challenging. Besides her exaggerated characters, she is constantly experimenting with style and plot structure. A truly innovative writer, she blends fantasy and realism and creates ghosts and gods with ease. The love of language and word play is apparent in all her writing. For all of these reasons, Virginia received the Hans Christian Andersen Award, one of the highest honors in the field of children's literature.

Virginia is also a teacher. She has held a distinguished visiting professorship at Queens College, and has also taught at Ohio State University.

Virginia's most important contribution to children's literature was to portray children discovering the value of their African American heritage and the uniqueness of their culture. Her books are about pride and courage. When she began writing in the 1960's, this was a new focus in children's books.

Virginia's readers tell her that her books teach them new ways of looking at life, and ways to survive hardships. "Having set out to be nothing more than a teller of tales, I have come to feel responsible— that what I have to say is more worthwhile than I had first thought."

Notes:

Page 125   "Ever after, the raised Black Fist..." Anne Commire, ed. *Something About the Author.* (Gale Research Co., 1989), vol. 56, p. 62

Page 126   "Thus they created..." Donald R. Gallo, ed. *Speaking for Ourselves* (National Council of Teachers of English, 1990), p. 90.

Page 127   "Ever after..., I have been..." Virginia Hamilton, *Paul Robeson* (Harper, 1974), p. x.

Page 132   "...just to remind myself..." Virginia Hamilton, "Writing the Source: In Other Words," *Horn Book Magazine* (December, 1978), p. 616.

"That's steady thinking..." Ibid.

Page 133   "Having set out..." Virginia Hamilton, "Newbery Award Acceptance," *Horn Book Magazine* (August, 1975), p. 343.

For further reading about Virginia Hamilton:

Gallo, Donald R., ed. *Speaking for Ourselves.* Urbana, Ill.: National Council of Teachers of English, 1990.

Haviland, Virginia, ed. *The Openhearted Audience.* Washington, D.C.: Library of Congress, 1980.

Mikkelsen, Nina. *Virginia Hamilton.* New York: Twayne Publishers, 1994.

Rollock, Barbara T. *Black Authors and Illustrators of Children's Books.* New York: Garland, 1988.

Books for Young Readers
by Virginia Hamilton

1967 Zeely

1968 The House of Dies Drear

1969 The Time-Ago Tales of Jahdu

1971 The Planet of Junior Brown

1972 W. E. B. Du Bois: A Biography

1973 Time-Ago Lost: More Tales of Jahdu

1974 M. C. Higgins, the Great

1975 Paul Robeson: The Life and Times of a Free Black Man

1976 Arilla Sun Down

1978 Justice and Her Brothers

1980 Dustland

1981 The Gathering

1982 Sweet Whispers, Brother Rush

1983 The Magical Adventures of Pretty Pearl

1983 Willie Bea and the Time the Martians Landed

1984 A Little Love

1985 Junius Over Far

1985 The People Could Fly

1987 The Mystery of Drear House

1987 A White Romance

1988 In the Beginning: Creation Stories from Around the World

1988 Anthony Burns: The Defeat and Triumph of a Fugitive Slave

1989 The Bells of Christmas

1990 Cousins

1990 The Dark Way: Stories from the Spirit World

1991 The All Jahdu Storybook

1992 Many Thousand Gone: African-Americans from Slavery to Freedom

1993 Plain City

1994 Jaguarundi

WALTER DEAN MYERS
High School Drop-out, College Graduate, Teacher

Four-year-old Walter Milton Myers learned to read from his foster mother's *True Romance* magazines. He entered school with a speech defect so severe only his family could understand him. A self-described "bad kid," he would have been expelled from the fourth grade if an appendectomy hadn't caused him to miss the last few weeks of school anyway. Walter's transformation from high school drop-out to highly respected author was a result of stubborn will power. His foster parents had great respect for hard work and education, and in spite of himself—their attitude rubbed off on Walter.

Walter Milton Myers was born in Martinsburg, West Virginia, on August 12, 1937. His parents, George and Mary Myers, had six children together, and were also raising George's two daughters from his first marriage.

When Walter was two years old, his mother died in childbirth. George Myers was left alone to care for eight children in a time when jobs for African-Americans were very scarce and low-paying.

When George's first wife, Florence, and her new husband, Herbert Dean, came to take Florence's two daughters back to Harlem in New York City to live with them, they offered to take Walter, too, and raise him as their son. The Deans never formally adopted him, but from then on Walter thought of them as his parents.

Florence and Herbert Dean were hard-working people who did their best to give Walter a good home. Herbert worked as a laborer, often holding two or three jobs at a time. He had very little schooling and was unable to read and write, but he gave Walter an important gift—a love of stories. Walter would sit on Herbert Dean's knee to hear him act out scary stories with great drama.

Herbert's father told Walter stories, too. Most of his were stories from the Bible. Whenever Walter misbehaved—missed Sunday school, wasted money, complained too much—his grandfather would tell a "God's gonna get you story" from the Old Testament, chosen to fit the occasion.

Florence Dean, Walter's foster mother, had no education, but she had managed to learn to read. She taught four year old Walter how to read by using romance magazines and *Classic Comics.*

Walter was unable to pronounce many sounds. The letters r, w, sh, and ch were especially difficult. To Walter, it was frustrating to be unable to speak so others could understand. It was very funny to many of his neighbors. They sometimes paid Walter to talk. When he entered school it was mistakenly decided he had a hearing problem, and he was fitted for hearing aids.

School was a trial for Walter, and he was a trial to his teachers. Because of his speech problem, he suffered cruel teasing from his classmates. His response was to lash out in rage, fighting with the other children, and defying authority. He once threw a book at a teacher he thought was patronizing him.

It was clear Walter was very bright. He was able to read before he began school, and his test scores were high. The speech defect made him miserable, however, and he was in constant trouble because of his behavior. His near-brush with expulsion in fourth grade resulted in his attending a different school the next year.

In fifth grade, Walter had a teacher who showed some insight into his difficulties. When she caught him reading comic books in class, she made up her mind to introduce him to some more serious literature. She brought a collection of good books to class for Walter and the other children to choose from. Walter especially liked an anthology of Norwegian folktales called *East of the Sun and West of the Moon.*

Walter's writing career began in fifth grade. The students were often required to read aloud. The teacher, recognizing Walter's speech problems, urged him to write what he read to the class. He wrote poems that avoided the sounds he had trouble pronouncing.

Although his writing was praised, it was the only area in which Walter had any success. He hated school and was frequently suspended. Suspension didn't bother Walter. He liked hanging out on the streets or in the park.

Walter also discovered the public library. He read as much as he could, devouring stories by Hemingway, E. M. Forster, and Dylan Thomas. These and others were his heroes. He wanted to know about their lives—what they wore, what they did each day. He would often go to the bar on Hudson Street where Dylan Thomas was known to spend much of his time. Walter would stand near the door and sometimes sneak inside for a look at Thomas.

"I thought Dylan Thomas was God."

The Harlem Walter grew up in was a neighborhood of joy and laughter, as well as a place of crime, drugs, and violence. It was a place where neighbors felt responsible for each other's children—scolding them, feeding them, caring for them. There were plenty of activities to keep children busy. The church sponsored basketball and baseball teams and dancing classes. Walter studied modern dance at his church—the same church where the Dance Theater of Harlem began. He had a starring role as Adam in a modern dance version of James Weldon Johnson's poem, "The Creation."

In junior high school, Walter's intelligence was recognized, and he was placed in a "Special Progress" program. This was an accelerated class which remained together for two years. These were Walter's most successful school years.

Walter attended Stuyvesant High School, which was known for academic achievement. His best subject was English. With his teacher's encouragement, Walter began to write short stories. The teacher praised his writing skills, and Walter considered the possibility of a writing career. His high school writing efforts won him a poetry prize and an essay contest.

In spite of his writing success, Walter was still not a good student. He was absent from school more than he was there, often spending his days in a park, reading or writing. Eventually, he dropped out of school without graduating.

During his high school years, Walter held several part-time jobs. He took a job as a delivery boy for a jewelry business to earn money for a used typewriter. Walter's foster father failed to see the value of writing stories, but he realized how much Walter wanted the typewriter, so he bought it for him.

Walter hoped that writing would provide his escape from the kind of life his Harlem neighbors led. These men ridiculed Walter's love of books and writing. They told him he was no better than they, and predicted he would end up a laborer like them.

Walter feared they might be right. He had not finished high school. Even if he had, there was no money for college. His books and his writing took him into a different world—away from the crime and violence that surrounded him, and the probability that his future would be spent in a series of menial jobs.

In 1954, Walter, then seventeen years old, was hanging out with other young men on the street—fighting and getting involved in gang disputes. Knowing this was a dangerous way to live, Walter considered his options. He needed a job—a good job if possible—but would require training. He decided to escape street life by taking one of the few routes open to him. He joined the Army.

If he was hoping to get some practical training while he was in the military, Walter was disappointed. He participated in war games, sat in foxholes for hours in the middle of the night, and was usually bored. After three years, at the age of twenty, he was discharged. Once again, with no skills or training, he needed to find a job.

Florence and Herbert Dean were now living in Morristown, New Jersey. After his discharge, Walter lived with them for a while and worked in a factory. He soon became restless and dissatisfied with that job, and returned to New York City, where he found a room to rent. He collected thirteen dollars a week unemployment benefits, and spent his days reading books. With hardly any money for food, he lost fifty pounds.

Eventually, a friend persuaded him to take the Civil Service Exam, and Walter got a job in the Post Office. Here he fell in love with a young woman named Joyce. They married in 1960.

While working at the Post Office, Walter also pursued a career as a writer. He wrote several short stories which were published in magazines that featured work by African Americans. He also tried his hand at poetry. His first published poem was written for his daughter, Karen, who was born in 1961.

Walter enrolled in a writing class and received encouragement from the teacher who recognized his talent. Walter had doubts, though. How could someone with no high school or college diploma be a successful writer? Still, he continued to earn praise from his teacher and to sell stories to magazines. His confidence in his writing ability grew.

Walter changed jobs frequently during the next few years. He had trouble settling down to be the kind of father he wanted to be to Karen and his son Michael Dean, who was born in 1963. Much of his time was spent in clubs where he played the bongos and drank with other young men who were also unsettled and directionless.

It was difficult for a man as bright and ambitious as Walter to be unable to find work other than short-term, unskilled jobs. The situation strained his marriage and made it more difficult to cope with the demands of raising two small children. Walter had some important points in his favor, though. He was a reader, which made him sure that the world was full of possibilities. He had always been encouraged by his parents and his teachers. Even in the worst of times Walter had goals to work toward, and knew he had the ability to achieve them.

In 1966, Walter found a job with the New York State Employment Service. He held two other part-time jobs at the same time. His wife Joyce was also working two jobs. Knowing their marriage was in trouble, they hoped a move to a better neighborhood would improve things. They bought a house in the Queens section of New York City.

Walter continued writing. It forced him to think about himself and his life. He still didn't think of himself as a professional writer, however. Although his short stories sold well, they certainly didn't earn enough money to support a family.

Walter still wanted to complete his education. He began taking night classes at City College in New York. For one and a half years he did very well, but he wasn't able to continue. He still worked two jobs to provide for his children. The move to Queens had not been enough to save his marriage. Walter and Joyce divorced.

Then, in 1968, Walter's writing career took a new direction. He saw an article in *Writer's Digest* magazine announcing a contest for African American writers sponsored by the Council on Interracial Books for Children. Walter had not thought of writing for children before, but he decided to give it a try. His story, *Where Does the Day Go?*, won first prize in the three to six year old category. In 1969 it was published as a picture book by Parents' Magazine Press.

Around this same time, Walter saw an advertisement in the newspaper for a writers' workshop at Columbia University to be led by John Oliver Killens, an African American novelist and founder of the Harlem Writers' Guild. Spurred by his recent success, Walter enrolled in the class. Killens was so impressed by Walter's writing talent he urged him to apply for an editorial position at Bobbs Merrill publishing house. Walter felt he was unqualified for the job. "I think they would have hired any Black who walked in the door. I walked in, they hired me," he said later.

Perhaps it was just a merely of good timing. More and more companies were responding to social and political pressures of the day. It was good business to have at least one African American on the payroll. However, Walter soon proved the was a valuable employee, not just a token of good race relations. At last he had a job that was challenging, and made use of his intelligence and abilities.

Walter's personal life was looking up again, too. He met and married Constance Brendel. In 1974 their son, Christopher, was born.

Walter remained with Bobbs Merrill for seven years, working as a senior trade editor. With determination and natural skill, Walter read and selected manuscripts, and edited them for publication. He learned how the publishing business worked, and what made a book salable.

Now in addition to his adult short stories for magazines, Walter was writing picture books for children. He adopted the pen name Walter Dean Myers to honor his foster parents, and he hired an agent.

The agent's job was to sell Walter's manuscripts to publishers. Walter had written a short story about young teenagers in Harlem. His agent showed it to an editor at Viking who thought it was a very good first chapter. Could she see an outline of the rest of the book? Quickly, Walter sat down and wrote an outline, turning his short story into a novel. *Fast Sam, Cool Clyde, and Stuff* was published in 1975, and was named an American Library Association Notable Book. Walter Dean Myers' career as a successful, award-winning author of young adult novels was launched. Two years later, Walter left his job at Bobbs Merrill and became a full-time writer.

Walter wanted to write for Black teenagers. He wanted them to be able to see themselves represented in books—not just in the background, but as main characters whose experiences and hopes and decisions were important. He knew that what makes people of all ages feel unhappy is a sense of isolation. He wanted to write books that would show his readers their own images and remove the feeling of being alone.

Walter Dean Myers' books portray young people supporting each other—laughing and crying together as they deal with serious issues such as death, drugs, sex, individual and group responsibility. The parents in his books are caring and responsible, though usually less than perfect. His female characters are strong. The peer groups are often interracial. All his characters have the same emotions and concerns as people anywhere. A major recurring theme in his work is that growing up Black in the inner city does not necessarily mean being downtrodden and impoverished.

In recent years, Walter Dean Myers has turned his attention to the need for biographical and historical works featuring Black Americans. He has added to his long list of novels for teenagers a biography of Malcolm X which won the Newbery Honor Award, a biography of Martin Luther King, Jr., an account of the courage and patriotism of an African American prisoner of war in Vietnam, and a history of the long struggle for freedom and civil rights.

The critics agree on several major strengths in Walter's writing.

They praise his use of dialogue, humor, drama, action, and believable characters. Three of his novels have won the Coretta Scott King Award, which is presented to a Black author for an "outstanding, inspirational, and educational contribution to literature." Five of his books have been named American Library Association Best Book for Young Adults. In 1994, Myers received the Margaret A. Edwards Award, which is given annually by the American Library Association's Young Adult Library Services Division. He has written about fifty books.

The Myers, who are grandparents now, live in Jersey City, New Jersey. In addition to his hobbies—photography and music (flute, guitar, and saxophone)—Walter likes to travel. He has been to Europe, Asia, Mexico, and South America. His travels have furnished settings and background information for several of his books.

In 1984 Walter fulfilled a long-held goal—he earned a bachelor's degree in communications from Empire State College. He now teaches a middle school writing course two days a month. He is a good teacher, who enjoys his work, and takes it very seriously. He also tries to write ten pages a day. He finds it easier to discipline himself this way than to work a certain number of hours every day.

In addition to calling upon his childhood and his travels for background material, Walter finds inspiration in the life and works of Langston Hughes and James Baldwin, highly respected African-American writers. Like them, he tries to depict the everyday lives of ordinary African Americans.

Notes:

Page 140   "God's gonna..." Rudine Sims Bishop, *Presenting Walter Dean Myers* (Twayne Publishers, 1991), p. 4.

Page 142   "I thought Dylan..." quoted by Roger Sutton, "Threads in Our Cultural Fabric," *School Library Journal* (June 6, 1994), p. 29.

Page 146   "I think they would..." quoted by Allen Raymond, "Walter Dean Myers: A 'Bad Kid' Who Makes Good," *Teaching Pre K-8* (October, 1989), p. 54.

For further reading about
Walter Dean Myers:

Bishop, Rudine Sims. *Presenting Walter Dean Myers.* Boston: Twayne Publishers, 1991.

___. "Profile: Walter Dean Myers." *Language Arts,* December 1990, pp. 862-866.

Raymond, Allen. "Walter Dean Myers: A 'Bad Kid' Who Makes Good." *Teaching Pre K-8*, October 1989, pp. 53-55.

Rollock, Barbara T. *Black Authors and Illustrators of Children's Books: a Biographical Dictionary.* New York: Garland, 1988.

Sutton, Roger. "Threads in Our Cultural Fabric." *School Library Journal,* June 6, 1994, pp. 24-29.

Zverin, Stephanie. "The Booklist Interview: Walter Dean Myers." *Booklist,* February 15, 1990, pp. 1152-1153.

Books for Young Readers
by Walter Dean Myers

1975   Fast Sam, Cool Clyde, and Stuff
1977   Brainstorm
        Mojo and the Russians
1978   It Ain't All for Nothin'
1979   The Young Landlords
1981   Hoops
        The Legend of Tarik
1982   Won't Know Till I Get There
1983   The Nicholas Factor
        Tales of a Dead King
1984   Motown and Didi
        The Outside Shot
1985   Arrow Adventure Series
1986   Sweet Illusions
1987   Crystal
1988   Fallen Angels
        Me, Mop, and the Moondance Kid
        Scorpions
1990   The Mouse Rap
1992   Mop, Moondance, and the Nagasaki Knights
        Now Is Your Time: The African American Struggle for
        Freedom
        A Place Called Heartbreak: A Story of Vietnam

The Righteous Revenge of Artemis Bonner
Somewhere In the Darkness
Young Martin's Promise
1993   Eighteen Pine Street Series
Malcolm X: By Any Means Necessary
1994   Darnell Rock Reporting
The Glory Field

GARY PAULSEN
Adventure Seeker

It was a cold wintry day in Minnesota. Gary walked down the street shivering. He had been in trouble at school. He had been picked on by his classmates again. Tired, discouraged, and half-frozen, he looked up at the lights shining in the windows of the library's reading room. He would go in, just to warm up a little.

When the librarian asked if he had a library card, Gary hesitated—he wasn't much of a reader. She handed him a registration form, urging him to complete it. Gary knew he was a misfit. He didn't have the right clothes. He was terrible at sports. His parents fought much of the time. Yet here was the librarian, offering him a library card as though none of that mattered. "When she handed me the card, she handed me the world. I can't even describe how liberating it was."

Gary Paulsen was born May 17, 1939, in Minneapolis, Minnesota. His father was an army officer, and was soon sent overseas to serve on General Patton's staff during World War II. His mother found work in a munitions factory in Chicago for the duration of the war and left Gary in the care of his grandmother, aunts, and babysitters. One babysitter was especially memorable for her total lack of interest his well-being. She didn't talk to him, play with him, or pay him any attention except to scold. Day after day, she would sit on the couch in the Paulsen living room listening to the radio. Day after day, Gary, only a toddler at the time, would sit and listen with her.

A frightening incident has remained in Gary's memory from childhood. At only four or five years old, he sneaked out of his apartment one day. In the alley between his building and the next, he was grabbed by a strange man and forced against the wall. In the nick of time Gary's mother came looking for him. She began to kick and punch the stranger, knocking him to the ground, and rescuing Gary.

Spending so much time listening to the radio gave Gary a large musical repertoire. When he was six or seven years old, his mother would take him to a neighborhood bar and stand him on a stool. Gary would sing the songs he learned on the radio. The bar's patrons would pay to hear their favorites. When they had collected enough money, Gary and his mother would go out to dinner.

In 1946, when Gary was seven, a message arrived from the father he couldn't remember. The war was over, and Gary's father wanted his wife and son to join him in the Philippines, where he was stationed with an army unit that was helping to rebuild the devastated country. When it came time to set sail, Gary and his mother traveled to California where they made arrangements to take a military ship to the Philippines. But Gary had to be smuggled aboard. He had the chicken pox, and it was against regulations to allow persons with contagious diseases on the ship.

The cruise was eventful. After several days alone in his cabin—recovering from the pox, and waiting for the tell-tale scabs to disappear Gary had run of the ship. He made friends of the crew, joining them in their quarters, and accepting chocolate bars as bribes from several who wanted to impress Gary's attractive mother. The sailors taught Gary to shoot dice, and rewarded him with a dollar if he rolled a winning number.

While at sea, there was a plane crash near the ship. Gary leaned over the rails, staring intently as people jumped off the sinking airplane to swim to rescue boats. Some made it safely, but many were attacked by sharks and wounded or killed. The survivors were taken aboard the ship where Gary's mother helped the ship's doctor treat the wounded. The ship sailed to Hawaii, where it left the crash survivors. Then they sailed on to Okinawa and the Philippines.

In the Philippines, the Paulsens had a house on the army base. The house was built three feet off the ground with walls only partway up to the ceiling. The design kept the house as cool as possible, but freely admitted insects. Often there were lizards on the ceiling. Gary's mother was warned not to chase them away—not only did they bring good luck, they ate the mosquitoes and flies.

Gary was the only child on the base. He had a tutor four days a week. The rest of his time he explored the base with the family's Filipino gardener as a companion. He played on rusted the Japanese tanks and the wrecked airplanes.

He found a homeless dog and adopted it. One evening when the family went to a party where there were other children, Gary accepted a dare and jumped down a flight of stairs. He landed with such force he bit off his tongue. He was rushed to the base hospital where the doctors reattached it. For two weeks he lived on powdered chicken soup mix drunk through a straw.

During the two years he lived in the Philippines, Gary saw things that were difficult for a child to understand. Many buildings had been destroyed in the war. There was a mass grave near the army base filled with victims of torture. Those who resorted to stealing to feed their starving families were severely punished. His confusion was made worse because he couldn't talk to his parents about the tragedies around him. They were struggling with their own problems. Both his parents drank too much and fought frequently. Gary's father was rigid and aloof. He only communicated with Gary to give him orders. Gary's mother disliked living in the Philippines. After two unhappy years she decided to go back to the United States with Gary.

Gary's father returned home soon afterwards. Together again, the family moved around constantly as his father was transferred from army post to army post. Gary found it hard to adjust to changing schools so often. He was shy and poor at sports. Making friends his own age was difficult, and getting along with his teachers was just as difficult. By the time he was in high school, Gary was in constant trouble for getting into fights and earning very poor grades. He skipped school most of his ninth grade year. At age fourteen, he ran away from home and traveled with a carnival. After returning, he had to do double the work in tenth grade in order to graduate on time.

Gary worked from the time he was in junior high school to buy clothes and to have spending money. He sold newspapers in hospitals and bars, and for a time was a pinsetter in a bowling alley.

Gary's home life continued to be unhappy. His father still drank to excess, and had terrible arguments with his mother. When things got too rough, Gary was sent to live with a relative to live. His grandmother and his aunts became critically important to him for the support they provided him during these years.

When Gary, a lonely and miserable teenager, walked into the library one winter day, his life changed. The librarian befriended him, introducing him to westerns and science fiction, and every now and then a classic. Gary read everything she gave him, taking the books home to the basement of the family's apartment house, where he passed his nights readings. The next summer he read a book a day. "It was as though I had been dying of thirst and the librarian had handed me a five-gallon bucket of water. I drank and drank."

From 1957 to 1958, Gary attended Bemidji College in Minnesota, paying for his first year by laying trap lines for the state. He caught what were considered to be predators and nuisance animals, such as coyotes and beavers, and collected bounties for them.

Gary was still unhappy and still prone to fight. He enlisted in the army in 1959, hoping the experience would help him straighten up. After initially fighting with his sergeant—and losing—Gary worked hard during his remaining three years in the service. At the end of his service he had earned the rank of sergeant.

Gary worked with missiles while in the army. After his discharge, he took extension courses and earned enough credits to become a field engineer. He then found employment in the aerospace industry working on guidance systems for anti-radar missiles. Gary didn't particularly like the job, although he was good at it. One day in 1966, during a slow period at work, Gary picked up a magazine and read an article on flight-testing new airplanes. It occurred to him that it would be wonderful to earn a living by writing about things he enjoyed. Then he thought about the reports he had written for his work. He had often made up whole sections of them. In a way, he already was a fiction writer.

That day Gary walked away from his job, telling his supervisor he was quitting to become a writer. He realized he didn't know anything about how to become a professional writer. But he thought of a way to learn. He would get a job working for a magazine.

Gary wrote a resume that made him sound qualified to be a magazine editor. He landed a job on a men's magazine in Hollywood, California, that published several well-known writers. It was soon obvious to his new employers that he knew nothing about magazines, but Gary convinced them he was serious about learning. He worked on the magazine for one year, mostly as a proofreader, and educated himself on how to become an author. "It was the best of all possible way to learn about writing. It probably did more to improve my craft and ability than any other single event in my life."

While learning on the job, Gary began his writing career. Every evening he wrote, and the next day he took taking his pages to work for his friends to read and evaluate. His first book, *The Special War,* based on interviews with Vietnam veterans, was published in 1966.

Gary also took advantage of his Hollywood location to do a little work in films. He played a bit part in a film called *Flap,* which starred Anthony Quinn. He appeared on screen for about thirty seconds. He also did some sculpting, and won a "best in show" prize at an art exhibit. He loved wood carving and thought he might even be able to earn a living at it. But writing was what he really wanted.

After a year at the magazine, Gary decided to leave California, where all the authors seemed to have the same writing style—one he felt uncomfortable with. He returned to Minnesota and rented a lake cabin. He didn't always have enough money to pay the rent, but the owners let him stay anyway. He trapped rabbits for fur to meet his expenses.

Gary's next book, *Some Birds Don't Fly*, was published in 1968. In 1969 *Mr. Tucket*, his first juvenile book, appeared. Then came seven years when he sold nothing. Gary had started drinking in 1968, and for five years he struggled with this disease, which had its origins in his childhood. In 1973, he won the battle over alcoholism and quit drinking.

On May 4, 1971, Gary married Ruth Ellen Wright, an artist he had met five years earlier while standing in line at a post office in New Mexico. Gary and Ruth had one son, James Wright. This was Gary's second marriage. He had a son and a daughter, Lance and Lynn, with his first wife.

To earn a living during these early years of his writing career, Gary worked at a number of different jobs, all of which gave him background material for his stories. Every night he worked at his writing. During the next twelve years, Gary wrote nearly forty books, over 200 magazine articles and short stories, and two plays. He wrote nonfiction about hunting, trapping, farming, animals, medicine, and outdoor life. He wrote juvenile and adult fiction—westerns, mysteries, and adventure stories. He won a bet with a friend by writing eleven short stories and articles in four days and selling them all.

Gary was compulsive about his work. Struggling to support his family at any job he could get, and writing during every spare minute, sometimes built up more stress than he could contain. When this happened he would walk around his Minnesota farm and shoot at hillsides with his rifle.

In 1976, Gary took courses at the University of Colorado, but he did not earn a degree. Most of his education was earned through the experience of daily living and from his reading.

1977 brought a dramatic change to the Paulsens' life. Gary published a novel called *Winterkill* and was sued for libel over its contents. The court case went on for months until it finally reached the State Supreme Court. Gary was vindicated, but was nearly bankrupt after paying the legal fees. He felt his publisher should have offered more support. The experience left him embittered with the publishing business. He decided he wanted nothing more to do with writing.

In 1980, Gary and Ruth moved to a remote cabin near the Canadian border in northern Minnesota. They had no electricity or running water, and while Ruth had her painting, Gary had no means of earning a living. He went back to trapping coyote and beaver for the state. Too poor to afford transportation, Gary ran his trap line on foot and on skis. It took him several days to cover the sixty-mile line. When a friend offered to give him four dogs and an old sled, Gary accepted. The dogs were slow, and Gary was completely inexperienced at this method of transportation, but it made his work easier.

Then one day, on his way back to the cabin after checking his lines, Gary found himself on a hill overlooking a frozen lake. He looked out over the crisp, sparkling snow and the vast expanse of ice, and was overcome by the beauty of this harsh winter land. He realized he couldn't bear the thought of returning to civilization just yet, and for seven days he ran his dogs over the glistening wilderness. Completely unequipped for the impromptu journey, Gary and the dogs ran sixty to seventy miles per hour all day long, sharing beaver carcasses from his traps when hungry, and huddling together for warmth at night. Ruth was frantic by the time he finally returned home, but Gary was trapped by the thrill of dogsledding. For the next five years, it became his obsession. "It was as if everything that had happened to me before ceased to exist. When I came off that seven-day run, I pulled all my traps, having resolved never again to kill."

When the friend who had given him the dogs told him about the Iditarod, a 1200-mile dogsled race across the interior of Alaska, Gary decided to enter. He had no idea what hardships he would be facing.

Gary needed more than his four old dogs for the race. He searched for a way to raise the money for the well-conditioned team he would need if he was to have any chance of completing the race. A publisher who had seen one of Gary's stories in a magazine called to ask him what he was writing now. Gary told him he was not writing at all— he was trying to raise enough money for the Iditarod. Sensing the makings of a good book, the publisher offered to send the necessary money if Gary would write about the experience afterward and allow him to publish it.

Motivated by his experience with the dogs, Gary was finally able to return to his writing. He published *Dancing Carl,* an unusual story which was first conceived as a ballet set to original music, and performed on public television in Minnesota. The next year *Tracker,* a novel about the relationship between the hunter and the hunted, and the acceptance of death, was published.

During the next months, Gary trained his dogs with the same

single-mindedness he had shown as a writer. He ran the dogs eighteen hours a day, seven days a week. They rested every four hours. During the rest periods, Gary sat huddled close to a fire with a pencil and paper, writing the story of an Eskimo boy taking a dog team across Alaska. The book, *Dogsong*, won a Newbery Honor Medal.

Gary ran his first Iditarod in 1983. It was a grueling race. For seventeen days he stood on the back of his sled, controlling his dogs by voice alone. The relationship between Gary and his dogs was crucial. If the lead dog sensed fear or uncertainty on Gary's part, she might not obey him. Dogs will sometimes stop running if they lose confidence in their driver. Sometimes they become uncontrollable, crashing the sled. The rules of the race were strict—Gary was allowed no help from anyone. Not even the television helicopters filming the race from above could come to the aid of a contestant in trouble. If he made a mistake, Gary knew he might die.

Running through the unbelievable beauty of the land that bordered the Arctic Circle, sometimes hallucinating from lack of sleep, Gary raced from the old mining town of Iditarod to Nome, on the shores of the Bering Strait. He came in forty-second in a field of seventy-three. Staggering across the finish line to greet his anxious wife and son, Gary announced he intended to win the next time.

In 1985, Gary raced again. This time he was not so lucky. A fierce wind caught the lead dogs and blew them right off the ground. The sled crashed on top of Gary, and in the trauma of the accident he suffered an angina attack. Recovering in the hospital, he was given a prognosis which left him deeply depressed. The doctors informed him that the damage to his heart made it impossible for him ever to consider running dogs again. Bereft, Gary called a friend and begged him to take the dogs and sled away immediately. He knew that if he came home to find them waiting for him he would be unable to resist taking them out again.

Despondent about his health and the end of his dogsledding days, Gary looked for a way to distract himself. On the west coast he chartered a small sailboat and headed out into the Pacific, intending to sail until completely exhausted. The new adventure had the opposite effect. The ocean air revived him, and left him feeling ready to face whatever challenges might lie ahead.

This craving for adventure has marked all of Gary's life, and has provided a rich source of material for his books. He experienced an emergency airplane landing in the Canadian bush, had battles with moose, and endured storms while sailing the Pacific with Ruth. He knows well what it is like to pack essential survival gear for a trek into the unknown and then lose it, and to be forced to survive by his own ingenuity and courage. *Hatchet* and *The Voyage of the Frog* are survival stories partly based on Gary's own experiences.

After returning from sailing the Pacific following his second Iditarod, Gary began to again focus his energies on writing. He threw himself into his work, writing for eighteen to twenty hours each day. The result of this intense commitment is a long list of books. In 1993, Gary's output included twelve new titles, a picture book illustrated by Ruth, several mysteries for eight to ten year olds, several books for teenagers, and *Eastern Sun, Winter Moon,* a memoir of his childhood written for an adult audience.

Gary likes to write for young people because he feels they are looking for newness and truth. He believes they are more open-minded than adults, and has a great deal of confidence in the young as a power for change and improvement.

Gary no longer writes with a pencil by a campfire. Now he takes his laptop computer with him on camping trips. Because the computer makes doing revisions so much easier, he polishes his work more, and feels his writing has improved.

Reviewers have always been impressed by the quality of Gary's writing. His books have earned comments like "uproariously funny," "side-splitting humor," "gripping adventure," and have won many awards, including the Central Missouri Award for Children's Literature, the Society of Midland Authors Award, Book of the Year designations from the New York Public Library and the American Library Association, and Newbery Honor Awards.

"It's like things have come full circle. I felt like nothing the first time I walked into a library, and now library associations are giving me awards. It means a lot to me."

In addition to writing prolifically, Gary finds time to give public readings and performances, and to do storytelling. One of his books, *The Madonna Stories,* written as a tribute to the grandmother and aunts who helped raise him, is intended to be performed before audiences. Gary reads some of the stories, and sings others to music written by the composer who collaborated with him on *Dancing Carl.*

Gary also works hard for nuclear disarmament causes. He believes that private citizens must take the initiative when governments fail to do so. With his son, he wrote a letter to the Soviet Writers Union in the late 1980's, and was invited to talk to a delegation of Russian writers in Minneapolis.

Gary and Ruth still have their cabin in northern Minnesota, as well as a historic adobe home in La Luz, New Mexico, and a two hundred acre ranch in Wyoming.

Notes:

Page 155   "When she handed me..." Anne Commire, ed., *Something About the Author* (Gale Research Co., 1989), vol. 54, p. 78.

Page 159   "It was as though..." Ibid.

Page 160   "It was the best..." Ibid., p. 80.

Page 163   "It was as if everything..." Ibid., p. 81.

Page 166   "It's like things have come..." Ibid.

For further reading about Gary Paulsen:

Gallo, Donald R., ed. *Speaking for Ourselves.* Urbana, Ill.: National Council of Teachers of English, 1990.

Paulsen, Gary. *Eastern Sun, Winter Moon.* New York: Harcourt Brace Jovanovich, 1993.

___. *Winterdance: The Fine Madness of Running the Iditarod.* New York: Bradbury Press, 1994.

___. *Woodsong.* New York: Harcourt Brace & Co., 1990.

Books for Young Readers
by Gary Paulsen

1968   Mr. Tucket
1976   Martin Luther King: The Man Who Climbed the Mountain
1977   The CB Radio Caper
        The Curse of the Cobra
        The Golden Stick
1978   The Night the White Deer Died
1980   The Spitball Gang
1983   Dancing Carl
        Popcorn Days and Buttermilk Nights
1984   Tracker
1985   Dogsong
1986   Sentries
1987   The Crossing
        Hatchet
        Murphy
1988   The Island
        Murphy's Gold
1989   The Madonna Stories
        Murphy's Herd
        Night Rituals
        The Voyage of the Frog
        The Winter Room
1990   The Boy Who Owned the School

Canyons

The Foxman

1991 The Cookcamp

Monument

The River

1992 A Christmas Sonata

The Haymeadow

Tiltawhirl John

1993 Harris and Me: A Summer Remembered

Murphy's Stand

Nightjohn

The Sisters Hermanas

1994 The Car

1995 The Tortilla Factory

The Culpepper Adventure Series: 1992 - 1994

Amos and the Alien

Amos Gets Famous

Amos's Last Stand

The Case of the Dirty Bird

Coach Amos

Cowpokes and Desperadoes

Dunc and Amos Meet the Slasher

Dunc and the Greased Sticks of Doom

Culpepper's Canyon

Dunc and Amos and the Red Tatoos

Dunc and Amos Hit the Big Top

Dunc and the Flaming Ghost

Dunc and the Haunted House

Dunc Breaks the Record

Dunc Gets Tweaked

Dunc's Doll

Dunc's Dump

Dunc's Halloween

Dunc Undercover

Legend of Red Horse Cavern

Prince Amos

The Wild Culpepper Cruise

SOURCES

The information in this book came from the references listed at the end of each chapter, and from the following sources:

Bishop, Rudine Sims. "Books from Parallel Cultures: Celebrating a Silver Anniversary." *The Horn Book Magazine* (March/April, 1993), 17-180.

Devereaux, E. "Publishers Weekly Interviews Gary Paulsen." *Publishers Weekly* (March 28, 1994), 70-71.

The Dictionary of Literary Biography. (Detroit: Gale Research Co., 1986).

Major Twentiety Century Writers: A Selection of Sketches from Contemporary Authors. (Detroit: Gale Research Co., 1991).

Paterson, Katherine. "Hope is More than Happiness." *New York Times Book Review.* (December 25, 1988).

_____ "Is There a Secret to Getting Published?" *The Writer* (July, 1992), 13-16.

Raymond, A. "Gary Paulsen—Artist With Words." *Teaching Pre K—8* (August/September 1992) 52-54.

Zola, M. "Profile of Jean Little." *Language Arts.* (January, 1981) 86-92.

INDEX

Photo Credits